# Everyday
# LAW
## *for Young Citizens*

A revised and expanded edition of the previously published book by Good Apple

**Written and revised by
Eric B. Lipson, J.D.
and
Greta Barclay Lipson, Ed.D.**

**Illustrated by Mark Gutierrez**

# Teaching & Learning Company
1204 Buchanan St., P.O. Box 10
Carthage, IL 62321-0010

*This book belongs to*

HAUKAP

Cover photos by Images & More Photography

Cover design by Peggy Larson

Cover art by Mark Gutierrez

Copyright © 2000, Teaching & Learning Company

ISBN No. 1-57310-242-3

Printing No. 98765432

**Teaching & Learning Company**
**1204 Buchanan St., P.O. Box 10**
**Carthage, IL 62321-0010**

# Dedication

To Bill and Lorene, our hearts' delight and inspiration.

# Acknowledgements

The authors wish to express their special appreciation to several people whose help enhanced the completeness of this book. John Bancroft of Troy High School, Troy, Michigan, spent many hours talking with us and providing background information on mediation. We thank him for the insights on a process on which he has unique expertise. We can see why John has earned the admiration of his students and his peers.

In addition, we would like to thank Richard Lenter, a peerless legal practitioner for generously sharing his expertise, practical experience and insights.

We would also like to thank Geraldine Barclay of the Fitzgerald Schools, Warren, Michigan; John and Barbara Bryant for their practical classroom advice and the mediators of Pattengill Elementary of the Ann Arbor Public Schools for sharing information on their conflict management program.

Finally, special thanks to Lorene Sterner for proofreading, editing and her excellent counsel, wisdom and patience.

# Table of

TLC10242 Copyright © Teaching & Learning Company, Carthage, IL 62321-0010

# Contents

# Dear Teacher or Parent,

Law touches our lives from the day of our birth to the day we die, from birth certificate to death certificate.

*Everyday Law for Young Citizens* supplies students with the basic principles of law in clear, straightforward language. Most importantly, *Everyday Law for Young Citizens* shows students how to examine legal issues in an analytical way. This approach helps students understand just what the U.S. constitutional system of justice is all about, how law resolves conflicts, how law balances the rights of the group and the rights of the individual within the group and how law applies to everyone equally.

*Everyday Law for Young Citizens* illustrates the importance of law. Without law there would be anarchy. Life would be a jungle with a constant series of day-to-day battles. Such existence is filled with insecurity and fear. Without law there is always the threat that someone bigger and stronger will come along and destroy or steal what we have worked so hard to build. Laws reflect and codify society's beliefs. The development of legal systems has allowed civilization to progress socially and technologically. In the words of Alexander Pope: "Order is Heaven's first law. And this confessed, some are, and must be, greater than the rest."

Law forms the foundation of civilization and rests on the bedrock premises of justice and fairness. In the United States there is an added requirement for laws. In our country and other democracies, laws are made by the people or by representatives elected by the people. That single fact separates free societies from totalitarian forms of government where kings, dictators or small groups of people make the laws. In the United States, we believe that allowing citizens to make laws in a free and democratic society is the highest and best form of government.

Because democracies rely on the will of the people, there is a special responsibility placed on citizens to participate in that government. To participate effectively, it is incumbent upon citizens to be educated about the issues of the day and about the way their government works. In the words of Thomas Jefferson: "If a nation expects to be ignorant and free . . . it expects what never was and never will be."

Sincerely,

Eric B. Lipson, J.D. and Greta Barclay Lipson, Ed.D.

# Preface to Everyday Law

Since people are fallible, the laws they make are often imperfect. Therefore, laws are changed to better reflect the times. Although it may never be possible to achieve "true and perfect justice," in the United States, we constantly strive to improve the law toward that ideal.

In our nation, laws change to reflect the progress and problems posed by advances in science, medicine, technology and human needs. To address this circumstance, *Everyday Law for Young Citizens* focuses on analyzing principles of law which are less variable from jurisdiction to jurisdiction and are less likely to undergo major changes. For that reason, we believe that *Everyday Law for Young Citizens* will be a valuable tool for teachers and students without fear that it will quickly become outdated. The authors hope that this book will contribute to the goal of helping students become responsible and informed citizens.

In the 12 years since *Everyday Law for Young Citizens* was first published in 1988, the world has undergone some revolutionary changes, especially in the area of information dissemination. In a word: the internet. In response, a small but significant part of this book has become a compendium of legal resources available on-line. References to helpful URLs are included both within the text and in a section at the end of the book.

The law, too, has evolved, but at a much slower pace. In fact, it is reassuring that all of the basic legal principles and most of the legal precedents cited in the first edition have remained good law. There have been changes, however. The area of student rights has been a dynamic one.

The rising spectre of school violence and social disorder has increased the challenge to preserve an orderly yet free society. Freedom of speech is always of prime importance in a free society as are the other guarantees in the Bill of Rights. The need to balance the rights of the individual and the needs of society at large is constantly evolving in the light of our living constitution.

In light of the recent epidemic of school violence, the topics of student rights, privacy and searches in school makes those topics covered in 1988 more relevant than ever. Rather than rewrite the "Case of the Unlucky Locker," which is still good law, we have added

several citations including a very interesting web site on searches by drug-sniffing dogs to add extra depth to the topic and a reference to the Veronia School athlete drug testing case.

Preventing school violence has become an urgent concern to teachers, administrators, parents and students. For that reason we have added a whole chapter on the topic of Peer Mediation. Peer mediation has proven itself to be an effective way to address conflicts and reduce violence in public schools. Although we cannot provide in a single chapter enough information for a school system to institute a mediation program, it is the authors' sincere hope that the material presented will provide the resources to do so. We are also including a statement made by John Bancroft before the U.S. Senate Education Subcommittee on his experience with peer mediation at Troy High School and the address of the John Marshall School of Law which provides assistance to those starting such programs.

In this revision, readers will see an expanded emphasis on role playing: mock trials, town hall meetings, mediations and even mock congressional sessions. These were done in response to feedback we received from teachers who found the role plays especially compelling and effective.

We have also updated the glossary to which we refer all readers. It may be an overstatement, but we feel that first mastering its language is the single most effective way to learn the law.

# A Word to the Teacher

The authors realize that most teachers using this book are not lawyers and may never have taught a law class.

Therefore, this book is designed to be an easy-to-use guide to legal principles and concepts for the lay person. The teacher needs only to follow the self-guided tour in order to lead the discussions and activities that logically flow from the cases. Succeeding cases build on one another and increase in sophistication. The only preparation needed should be reading each chapter before class.

We hope that the benefits of learning law extend to everyday classroom behavior and situations. The exercises are designed to promote peer mediation as a tool for peaceful resolution of conflicts before they boil over into violence. Interested teachers and parents, whether lawyers or not, can use this book to enhance these vital skills which will help students survive and thrive in the uncertain world of tomorrow.

# Guide to the Format of the Book

"Basic Principles of Law" outlines information in question-and-answer form.

"Case Study" sets the stage with a realistic scenario.

"What's Your Opinion?" follows each case and asks for student opinion. Each opinion question is followed by "The Law Says" which provides the current status of the law.

"What If?" poses variations on the theme calling for more informed student opinion. When appropriate, "What If?" questions will be followed by an "Answer."

"Activities" suggest optional writing, discussion and role play possibilities and spin-offs of the case.

"Glossary" defines legal words and phrases in the text.

Bibliographic guide to internet legal resources.

"Appendix" includes the U.S. Constitution and testimony of John Bancroft to the U.S. Senate Subcommittee on Education on the topic of Peer Mediation.

# Opening Discussion

1. Why do you think we need laws?

2. Why are laws important?

3. How do laws lubricate the wheels of society?

4. What would daily life be like without laws?

# What Laws Do

Laws balance the rights of individuals and the good of the community.

Laws are designed to apply to everyone equally, no matter what age, race, religion, national origin, sex or income.

The law establishes the rules of fairness.

Laws help people resolve conflicts peacefully. Laws guarantee that people receive "due process," which means that everyone is entitled to a fair hearing or trial before they are penalized or deprived of freedom, life or property.

Laws incorporate and express social values and ethics.

The goal of law is to protect the health, safety, freedom and well-being of all citizens.

# Basic Principles of Law

**Question:** What are laws?
**Answer:** Laws are rules of conduct.

**Question:** What do laws do?
**Answer:** Laws maintain order and promote public welfare.

**Question:** What are the two main branches of law?
**Answer:** Criminal law and civil law.

## Criminal Law

**Question:** What is criminal law?
**Answer:** Criminal law is the branch of law concerned with defining crimes and enforcing criminal laws.

**Question:** What is a crime?
**Answer:** A crime is a socially unacceptable or destructive act punishable by a fine and/or imprisonment. Some crimes are even punishable by death.

**Question:** Who can prosecute a person accused of a crime?
**Answer:** Only a government prosecutor can prosecute criminal offenses. Although a private person can file a complaint, the prosecutor decides whether or not to prosecute.

**Question:** What is a misdemeanor?
**Answer:** A misdemeanor is a less serious crime, usually punishable by less than one year in prison (and/or a fine).

**Question:** What is a felony?
**Answer:** A felony (also known as a "high misdemeanor" in some states) is a more serious crime, punishable by over one year in prison (and/or a fine). The most serious felonies ("capital crimes"): murder, treason and kidnapping) are punishable by death in some states.

**Question:** If a person charged with a crime claims to be innocent, how is his guilt or innocence decided?

**Answer:** Innocence or guilt is decided in a legal procedure known as a trial. The accused person has the choice of a trial by a judge or a trial by a jury.

**Question:** What if a defendant cannot afford an attorney?
**Answer:** Then the government must appoint and pay for an attorney for the defendant.

**Question:** How certain must a judge or jury be that the defendant committed the crime before they can find the defendant guilty?
**Answer:** To convict the defendant, the fact finder (judge or jury) must decide that the defendant is guilty "beyond a reasonable doubt." This is a very high standard of proof, meaning that there must be very little doubt that the accused person is guilty.

**Question:** Must criminal laws be in writing? If so, why?
**Answer:** Yes. Criminal laws must be clearly written so that people will know in advance what acts are illegal.

**Question:** If a person is charged with a crime, does the law presume that that person is innocent or guilty before trial?
**Answer:** The law presumes that a defendant is innocent until proven guilty beyond a reasonable doubt.

**Question:** What other rights do criminal defendants have in the United States?
**Answer:** The right to a public trial. The right to call witnesses at trial. The right to cross-examine witnesses brought by the prosecution. Defendants also have a right to appeal their cases to a higher court if they lose at trial and believe the lower court erred.

# Civil Law

**Question:** What are civil laws?

**Answer:** Civil laws are the noncriminal rules that define people's civil rights and civil responsibilities and allow them to enforce those rights.

**Question:** What remedies can civil laws provide if a person's civil rights are violated?

**Answer:** Courts can order people who violate other people's rights (or who injure other people or breach contracts) to pay money to those they injure. Courts can also issue orders to force people to live up to their legal responsibilities. Courts can also issue orders called injunctions to forbid parties from injuring people or property in the future.

**Question:** What standard of proof must a plaintiff (the person making the complaint) reach in order to win a lawsuit?

**Answer:** To win a civil lawsuit, the plaintiff must prove his or her case by a preponderance of the evidence. This means that the scales of justice must tip in favor of the plaintiff by any amount.

# Differences Between Civil and Criminal Law

**Question:** What are the major differences between civil and criminal law?

**Answer:**
1. Only the government can prosecute criminal cases. But any person or organization can file a civil lawsuit in court.
2. The standard of proof necessary to convict a criminal defendant (beyond a reasonable doubt) is much higher than the standard necessary to win a civil suit (a preponderance of the evidence).
3. Criminal defendants do not have to testify at their trial if they choose not to (see the Fifth Amendment). Defendants in civil lawsuits may be required to testify.
4. Violations of criminal law can be punished by fines, imprisonment or even death. Violations of civil laws cannot be punished by imprisonment (unless one violates a court order) and certainly not death!

# Lawmaking

**Question:** Who makes the laws?
**Answer:** In the United States laws are made by the people or their elected representatives.

**Question:** How are laws made?
**Answer:** Sometimes people vote on laws directly in a vote known as a referendum. Most laws are proposed and enacted by representatives elected by citizens of voting age. The function of the legislative branch is to make laws and hold fact-finding hearings.

**Question:** What is the name of the legislature of the United States government in Washington, D.C.?
**Answer:** The Congress. The U.S. Congress is bicameral (made up of two houses). In the Senate, each state is represented by two senators. In the House of Representatives, states are represented based on their populations.

**Question:** Do states have legislatures?
**Answer:** Yes. Every state has a state legislature. Some states have unicameral legislatures, some bicameral.

**Question:** What are the legislative branches of local governments?
**Answer:** Cities, towns, counties, townships, parishes, etc., have councils, commissions and boards.

# Law Enforcement

**Question:** What branch of the government enforces and carries out the law?
**Answer:** The executive branch carries out the laws passed by the people and the legislature. Law enforcement is also a function of the executive branch.

**Question:** Who is the chief executive of the United States?
**Answer:** The President.

**Question:** What is the name of the chief executive of a state?
**Answer:** The governor.

**Question:** Who is the chief executive of a city or town?
**Answer:** The mayor is the most common top executive for cities.

12

# Judging the Law

*Question:* What branch of the government interprets the laws when there is a disagreement whether a law has been broken?

*Answer:* The judicial branch (the courts).

*Question:* What is the highest court in the United States?

*Answer:* The United States Supreme Court is the highest court. Nine justices sit on the Supreme Court which is headed by the Chief Justice. All decisions must be by a majority of justices.

# Discussion Questions

1. Why do you think that the founders of the United States chose to separate the powers of government into three different branches? Wouldn't a single branch be more efficient?
2. The English statesman, Lord Acton wrote, "Power tends to corrupt. Absolute power corrupts absolutely." What did he mean? Do you think this philosophy had an influence on our country's founders?

# Constitutional Law

*Question:* What is the Constitution?

*Answer:* The Constitution of the United States is the supreme law of the land. It is the blueprint for the government. It was written in 1787 with 26 amendments added since then.

*Question:* What does the Constitution do?

*Answer:* It creates the different branches of government and defines their powers. It guarantees the rights of the people.

*Question:* What form of government does our Constitution create?

*Answer:* First of all, our government is a democracy. That means that all power of the government is granted by the people. Second, it is a Federal Republic, dividing government between the central government in Washington, D.C., and the individual state governments.

*Question:* What type of democracy is created by the Constitution?

*Answer:* A representative democracy. The people elect representatives whose opinions agree with theirs.

*Question:* If a law or an act by an official violates the Constitution, what word describes that violation?

*Answer:* Laws or acts that violate the Constitution are called "unconstitutional" and are, therefore, invalid, void and legally unenforceable.

# Bill of Rights

*Question:* What is the Bill of Rights?

*Answer:* Over the years, additions and corrections to the Constitution have been made. These changes are known as amendments. The first 10 amendments are known as the Bill of Rights. They define the rights of the individual and limit the power of the government over the people.

Throughout this book, there are references to the amendments. They should be read to and discussed when they are referred to in the text.

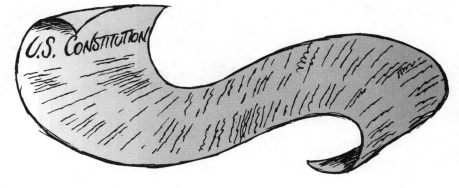

# Opening Activity

Here is an activity just for the fun of it. If it is true that the law touches everything we do from the moment we are born until we die, let's try to prove that statement. Picture yourself, as a newly born baby, in the center of a diagram with a web of people and events surrounding your arrival. List the ways in which the law is woven into the fabric of your life from the very first day of your life.

There are legal processes and documents all along the way. A baby is delivered in a licensed hospital by licensed doctors and nurses. The hospital building itself was designed by a licensed architect who must obey zoning and building codes. The infant is registered on a legal birth certificate and is a legal citizen of the state and the USA. Mother and child are driven home by a licensed driver who must obey traffic laws. Baby is welcomed home by the licensed family dog who bounds out of the family home or apartment which is owned or rented under a legal contract. Baby is cuddled by a sister or brother who may run an errand for the new family member on a licensed bike to the local drugstore which is licensed to dispense medicine, with a registered pharmacist on duty. As the child grows she may attend a daycare center whose rules are written by the government and, of course, attend a school (again, built to strict codes) and taught by certified teachers.

The list never ends. Law is pervasive and important in every aspect of our lives.

# Assault and Battery
## Case of the School Girl Scuffle

Carol Cruncher and Molly Meek had never been what you would call friends. In fact, you might call them enemies since Molly was now dating Carol's ex-boyfriend, Howie Hunk.

One day after school, Carol Cruncher walked up to the corner where Molly Meek was talking to some friends. Cruncher was steaming.

"I should break your arm for stealing my boyfriend," she hissed.

"What do you mean, steal?" Molly shot back. "Howie decided to stop seeing you because you are such a motor-mouth."

"Who's a motor-mouth? Nobody can call me names and get away with it! I'm going to slap some sense into you right now," said Cruncher, stepping forward menacingly, hand upraised.

It was a frightening move and Molly Meek was really scared. She stepped away without looking, stumbled backward and fell off the curb into the street. She hurt her arm in the fall and broke her brand-new watch.

"Look at what you've done," moaned Molly in tears. "You deliberately made me fall. Now you're in trouble. You're responsible for my arm and my watch!"

"Oh no I'm not," Cruncher smirked. "I never even touched you. Everybody could see that. And even if I did, you really had it coming for calling me a big mouth."

**"Nobody can call me names and get away with it!"**

# What's Your Opinion?

1. Did Carol Cruncher violate the law by threatening to strike Molly?

**The Law Says:** Yes. Carol's threat was an assault. An assault is defined as "an immediate threat of physical harm when the victim reasonably believes that the attacker is about to carry out the threat." Although the terms *assault* and *battery* are often used interchangeably, technically the assault is the threat or attempt. The battery is the actual physical contact.

2. Is any harmful physical contact with another person, without permission, a battery if it is done intentionally?

**The Law Says:** Yes. Any hurtful or harmful touching without permission is a battery, if done intentionally or through recklessness.

3. Are assault and battery violations of the criminal and/or civil law?

**The Law Says:** Both. Minor assault and battery is a criminal misdemeanor. Serious assault and battery (with a weapon or one that causes serious injury) is a felony. One can also bring a civil lawsuit against an attacker to collect damages caused by the attack or obtain an injunction to forbid future attacks.

4. Can a verbal insult ever justify hitting someone?

**The Law Says:** No. The law does not consider that an insult can justify a physical assault.

5. Is Carol Cruncher responsible legally for Molly's injured arm and broken watch?

**The Law Says:** Yes. Even though Carol Cruncher didn't touch Molly Meek, Carol's threat was an assault which caused the injury to Molly.

# What If?

1. **What If** Carol Cruncher spit in Molly's face? Would that be assault and battery? Explain.

**Answer:** Yes. This is a case of assault and battery. Even though spitting is not a strong physical contact, it is still considered a battery. In defining a battery, the law does not indicate the degree of force that must be used, nor does it indicate what the striking must be done with. (See also answer 4.)

2. **What If** the assault and battery were committed with a baseball bat or a rock? Does this make a difference?

**Answer:** Yes. Because these objects can create more serious injuries. Such an attack could be considered "assault with a deadly weapon," which is a felony–a more serious crime carrying greater penalties.

3. **What If** the two girls were arguing in the school yard and Carol Cruncher pulled a toy gun out of her pocket that looked like the real thing, and said, "I'm going to blow your head off!" Molly, terrified, fainted on the sidewalk. Is this an assault?

**Answer:** Yes. Even though the weapon was a toy, if Molly reasonably believed it was real, this would be an assault. In some states it could even be considered an assault with a deadly weapon!

4. **What If** Carol calls Molly a nerd and Molly, enraged, takes a swing at Carol but misses entirely? Was Molly guilty of assault?

**Answer:** Yes. Though a minor assault which causes no damage would probably not be prosecuted by the police, or result in civil damages, such behavior could merit disciplinary action by a teacher or principal.

5. **What If** two people are arguing and one person gets so upset that he swings his fist and knocks off the other person's eyeglasses? Is this an assault and battery even if the striking party never physically touched the face of the person wearing the glasses?

**Answer:** Definitely yes. This is an assault and battery. Eyeglasses, clothing, jewelry and any other objects worn by a person are considered to be part of the body as far as the law of assault and battery is concerned.

6. **What If** Carol Cruncher backs Molly into a corner and there is no way out? Carol takes a swing at Molly. To ward off the attack, Molly lashes out and swings back hard, knocking Cruncher to the ground. Is Molly guilty of assault and battery?

**Answer:** No, Molly is not guilty. The law recognizes that self-defense is appropriate to protect oneself or others from attack. Self-defense is the only justification that the the law recognizes as a defense to assault and battery. And once the threat is gone, the justification of self-defense is no longer available.

7. **What If** Molly grabbed a baseball bat to protect herself and smacked Carol. Is that self-defense?

**Answer:** Not unless Carol also had a bat. It is important to remember that one may not use more force in self-defense than absolutely necessary to repel the attack. A bat is a dangerous weapon and by using it Molly was raising the level of violence inappropriately.

# Activities

1. Are there other ways to settle the problems between Carol Cruncher and Molly Meek that could be tried instead of filing a lawsuit or a criminal complaint? (See the following chapter on Peer Mediation.)

2. If you were given the task of establishing a Peer Mediation Center to help students resolve conflicts and work things out constructively, how would it be organized? How could peer advisors be used along with adults? Write a paragraph or a page describing such a program. What could the people in such a center do to resolve conflict and avoid violence?

3. Hold a panel discussion on violence in school. What forms does it take? What do you think the causes are? How can the problems be reduced?

# Peer Mediation
## Case of the Non-Scuffle

Let's play back the "Case of the School Girl Scuffle" to the point just before Molly trips and imagine a different outcome using a program of conflict management called Peer Mediation that aims to stop violence before it begins.

"I'm going to slap some sense into you," said Cruncher, stepping forward toward Molly, menacingly, hand upraised.

"Hey! Stop, stop, stop!" boomed a friendly but firm voice.

"Whoa! Hold it!" came a higher but equally authoritative voice. Both girls looked over as two figures emerged from the crowd. Carol Cruncher's raised hand lowered to her side.

Moose Martin, captain of the football team, and Humaira Gupta, President of the Asian Students Association, came running over. Humaira, small as she was, stood between the quarreling girls.

"Don't get suspended for fighting," said Humaira quietly to both girls. "And no one wants to get hurt."
"Molly's a loser," shot out Carol.

"Witch!" spat Molly.

"You'll both be losers if this goes any further," said Moose.

"You can both be winners if that's what you want," added Humaira.

"Why don't we go mediate this right now and try to work it out?" said Moose. "And remember: Rule 1: NO NAME CALLING."

"OK, OK," said Carol. It was hard to say no to two of the most respected students in the school. "But I want Holly Hoopster to be one of the mediators."

"No problem," said Moose. I saw her in study hall."

"Humaira and Holly are fine with me," said Molly.

# Peer Mediation
## Case of the Non-Scuffle

Later that afternoon Molly and Carol, along with the mediators, emerged from the mediation room. All the parties shook hands. Carol and Molly weren't smiling, but neither were they fighting.

"I have your agreement in this envelope," said Humaira. "Remember, it's just between us and nobody else."

"Right," said Molly and Carol together. Everyone knew that mediations were private and confidential.

"Good job, both of you." added Holly, "I'm proud of you for working this out." Both Molly and Carol smiled, if uneasily, at the compliment.

"Thanks," said Carol. "I admit, I do feel better."

"Thanks for being so brave." said Molly to the tiny Humaira who had stepped between them.

"No problem," said Humaira, smiling broadly.

Everyone breathed a sigh of relief that another potential fight had been avoided.

# Peer Mediation

*Note to the teacher: This chapter is slightly different in structure than all of the others. That is because mediation is a different process than the legal process. Mediation helps resolve problems before they become legal problems.*

**Question:** What is peer mediation?

**Answer:** Peer mediation is a voluntary process for conflict management in which students in conflict meet with trained student mediators to resolve their problem in a mutually agreeable fashion. When a solution is agreed upon by the parties, the mediators put it in writing and all the parties sign to show their acceptance.

**Question:** What are the steps in peer mediation?

**Answer:** Parties are referred to mediation by themselves or other students, a teacher, administrator, parent or any interested person when a conflict arises.
1. Parties agree to mediate their problem with peers.
2. Parties agree on two mediators.
3. Parties agree to try to find a solution.
4. Parties agree to the following rules:
   a. No interrupting.
   b. No name calling or making faces or gestures.
   c. Be honest.
   d. Agree to a solution and stick to it.
   e. Keep the entire problem and the solution private.

**Question:** Who can be peer mediators?

**Answer:** Anyone who is willing to do the following:
1. Be a good communicator: to listen, respond, suggest.
2. Be fair. Don't blame anyone or pre-judge a situation.
3. Be trustworthy and not violate confidentiality.
4. Act in a mature way—be sensitive, responsible, caring and especially levelheaded.
5. Respect all parties.

**Question:** Why is it important to have a diverse group of mediators?

**Answer:** An important part of a successful peer mediation program ensures that mediators are drawn from every group in the school so everyone feels represented.

**Question:** What do peer mediators do?

**Answer:**
1. Listen carefully.
2. Repeat or paraphrase what is said by the parties.
3. Ask questions that will help the parties come to a solution.
4. Encourage good ideas.
5. Be respectful of all parties.
6. Help the parties come up with their own solution.

# Peer Mediation

**Peer Mediators Do Not:**
1. Laugh or make fun of anyone.
2. Treat people like they are stupid.
3. Ignore anyone's ideas.

*Question:* Why does peer mediation work?

*Answer:*
1. The solution comes from the disputants, not teachers or adults.
2. Mediators come from all groups in the school.
3. Mediators are leaders.
4. Mediation and peaceful conflict resolution become part of the culture of the school.
5. Disputants feel that the process is fair.
6. The program teaches students problem-solving skills.
7. It reduces tensions in the school as a whole.
8. People learn to see others' points of view, and it prepares students to live peacefully in a diverse community.

# Activities

**Role Play:** Assign students to play the parts of Carol and Molly and the two mediators, Humaira and Holly. Carry out a mediation in front of the class. After coming up with a mediated solution, have one of the mediators write it down and have the mediators, "Molly" and "Carol" sign it.

Typical conflicts which can be role-played are: abusive language to peers, gossip or alleged gossip, threats, damage to others' property, neglecting to return borrowed items, boyfriend-girlfriend disputes and physical altercations.

# Negligence/Tort Law
## Case of the Bicycle Blunder

**She put her foot through the spoke of Klutz's front wheel.**

Claude Klutz pulled up to the supermarket on his new Motocross bike. In a hurry as usual, he ignored the bike rack and left it laying on the sidewalk, right smack in front of the automatic doors.

Bustling out of the store carrying three big bags, came Greta Golightly, whose arms were loaded. She could not see over her groceries and certainly couldn't see the bike lying in her path. Nor did she expect to encounter any obstruction lying on the sidewalk that would interfere with foot traffic in and out of the store. Before she realized what had happened, she had put her foot through the spokes of Claude's front wheel.

Groceries went flying everywhere and so did Ms. Golightly. Claude Klutz heard the commotion on his

way out and saw a woman sprawled on the ground on top of his wrecked bike!

"You've ruined my wheel! Why did you do that?" he yelled.

"I just about killed myself on your bike and that's all you have to say?" she shouted back, stumbling to her feet. "How about saying 'I'm sorry'?"

"You owe me for a new wheel," Claude insisted.

"Wrong, Pal! You owe me for all these ruined groceries, and you might owe me for a broken leg," countered Greta, limping badly.

# What's Your Opinion?

1. Who is wrong in this case? Explain.

**The Law Says:** Claude Klutz is wrong. His wrongful act is legally known as a tort (*tort* means "wrong" in French). Claude has committed a tort because 1) he had a duty to Greta (to be careful) and 2) his breach of that duty caused harm to Greta. *Negligence* means Claude neglected his duty to be reasonably careful. *Negligence* is the legal word for *carelessness*. Claude's negligence makes him liable (responsible) for Greta's damages caused by that negligence.

2. What duty did Claude have to Greta Golightly in this case?

**The Law Says:** Claude had a duty to Ms. Golightly and all other people who could reasonably be expected to be shopping. His duty was to park his bike carefully so that it was out of the way.

3. Must Greta Golightly pay for the damage she did to Claude's bike?

**The Law Says:** No. Greta is not liable (responsible) in this case because she was not negligent. She had no responsibility to avoid a bike that should not have been there in the first place. But it is arguable that Greta did contribute in a small way to the accident by not looking which could reduce Claude's liability.

4. What is Greta's duty in this case?

**The Law Says:** Greta has the duty which we all have all of the time: the duty to be reasonably observant and reasonably careful.

5. Can Claude Klutz be held responsible for Greta Golightly's injuries even if he is a minor?

**The Law Says:** Yes. Minors can be held responsible for their torts if the court finds that they were old enough to know better (to know they should have been more careful under the circumstances, given their age and experience).

6. If Claude has no money, how can Greta collect from him for her damages?

**The Law Says:** In some states Claude's parents might be held responsible for Claude's negligent behavior. (See "Case of the Beer Bust.") Also, if Greta sues Claude and wins, the judgment (decision in her favor) can be good for 10 years or more, so when Claude gets a job or if he wins the lottery, Greta can collect.

7. Claude has committed a tort. A tort is a civil wrong. Is Claude Klutz also guilty of a crime?

**The Law Says:** No. In this case, Claude's act is not a crime because it was not done intentionally or recklessly. It was an accident caused by carelessness.

8. Can a wrongful act be both a tort and a crime? Under what circumstances?

**The Law Says:** Yes. Some wrongful acts can be both a civil tort and a crime if they are done intentionally or very recklessly. Intentional torts are more serious than negligent torts. Such acts can be prosecuted criminally and also pursued in a civil lawsuit.

9. Assault and battery, malicious destruction of property and sometimes trespassing are intentional torts that are also crimes. Why do you think intentional torts are considered more serious than negligent torts?

**The Law Says:** When someone injures a person or their property by accident, it is not considered as mean or dangerous an act as when someone intentionally tries to do harm or when their recklessness causes harm.

# What If?

1. **What If** Claude is riding his bike carefully on the street and Greta Golightly steps off the curb into his path without looking? Claude hits her, damaging his bike and Greta's groceries. Who is negligent then? Why?

**Answer:** In that case, Greta is negligent. She neglected her duty to look both ways before walking into the street. Claude was not negligent if he was operating his bike safely since he had the "right of way" and would not expect Greta to walk off the curb without looking. Greta has committed the tort in this case.

2. **What If** Claude is riding his bike down the street on a clear, sunny day? Suddenly, a surprise gust of wind blows his bike off course and he strikes Greta who was crossing the street several feet away. Would either party be responsible to pay for the other's damages? Why?

**Answer:** In this case, neither party is responsible. Since the gust of wind was an unforeseeable surprise, there is no negligence by either party and therefore no tort and no liability by either.

# Activities

1. We are all responsible for our own behavior. We all have a duty to be reasonably careful to avoid injuring other people or their property. List the duties a reasonable person would have while doing the following:

   riding a bicycle or skateboard
   playing on the playground
   driving an automobile
   cooking food in a restaurant
   delivering papers in a neighborhood
   shooting a BB rifle
   playing football, baseball, hockey, soccer, etc.
   building a tree house
   inviting people into your home
   going swimming
   repairing a friend's bicycle

# Activities

2. A local storekeeper, Mr. Mercantile, is sick and tired of the kids leaving their bikes outside the entrance to the store after school and being rowdy in the store. Their bikes block the way so other customers can't get in and other customers stay away when students are "hangin' out" in his store. Angrily, the storekeeper posts a sign on the door that reads: "Absolutely No Students Allowed Until After 5:00 p.m." Some of the students just grumble but others want to do something constructive about the problem.

**Question:** Can Mr. Mercantile legally restrict students from entering his store?
**Answer:** Yes, as long as he is not discriminating on the basis of race or sex or national origin or religion. In other words, if he said, for example: "No female students allowed," he would be in violation of the civil rights laws.

Role-play a scene with the student making a plan. How can they negotiate with Mr. Mercantile so that they may be permitted to shop in the store after school?

# Contracts
# Case of the Heavy Chevy

Fabulous Frankie Farbush had just turned 16, and the very first thing he did on this birthday was apply for a driver's license. On his way back home, Frankie spotted a really sweet old Chevy parked in the driveway of the Hardnose house. It had a big "for sale" sign in the windshield. Frankie fell madly in love with it. He knocked on the door of the house and Harriet Hardnose answered. She explained that she wanted $1000 for the car and it was a real bargain. Frankie almost passed out with excitement and shouted, "It's a deal!" At that moment he was positive he could manage the finances. Hardnose said she wanted a deposit to hold the car. She wrote a contract which read:

> Sold by Harriet Hardnose to Frankie Farbush for $1000, her red Chevrolet. A nonrefundable deposit of $50 will hold the car for seven days at which time Farbush will pay the $950 balance and Hardnose will transfer the title (complete the sale).

They both signed and dated the agreement. Frankie gave her $50.00–all his savings. Frankie made his way back home, dizzy with the thrill of it. Wait until his friends see him in that vintage car! He would work and slave to pay for the car. Maybe his dad would help him. As he approached his house, a cloud of doubt began to descend. When Frankie told his parents what he had done, his father was furious. They rushed back to the Hardnose place where his dad demanded the $50 deposit be returned.

"A deal is a deal," Hardnose reminded him. "Look at what it says in the contract: *nonrefundable*. Frankie signed it. I'm sorry, but I'm keeping the deposit for my trouble. Besides, right after Frankie left, another customer turned up who wanted to pay cash. I could've sold it on the spot. But I lost the chance on account of the deposit!"

"A deal is a deal. I'm keeping the deposit."

**"A deal is a deal. I'm keeping the deposit."**

# What's Your Opinion?

1. What is a contract?
**The Law Says:** A contract is a legally binding agreement between two or more people (or businesses), exchanging one thing of value for another.

2. Did Harriet Hardnose and Frankie Farbush enter into a contract?
**The Law Says:** Yes. Frankie agreed to pay $1000 in exchange for Harriet selling him the car.

3. Was the contract valid and enforceable? Explain.
**The Law Says:** No. Since Frankie was under 18, he was not yet legally an adult. As a minor, he could not enter into an enforceable contract.

4. Must Harriet return Frankie's deposit?
**The Law Says:** Yes. Contracts with minors are voidable by the minor or his parents, and since Frankie's father made Frankie void the contract, Ms. Hardnose has no legal right to keep the money. (*Void* means "to have no legal effect, as if the contract never existed.")

5. What is it called when one party breaks a valid contract or does not live up to his end of a bargain?
**The Law Says:** Failure to perform, in whole or in part, is called a "breach of contract."

6. Can a contract be oral?
**The Law Says:** Yes. Contracts for small amounts of money and which can be carried out in less than a year can be valid even if they are not in writing. Some contacts, however, such as land sales contracts, are not valid unless they are in writing.

7. What kinds of problems arise with oral contracts?
**The Law Says:** Oral contracts are hard to enforce because it is hard to determine exactly what the terms are. It is often hard to prove that the contract even existed if one of the parties contests it. It is always a good idea to put any agreement into writing to avoid confusion and misunderstanding.

8. Did Frankie Farbush breach a contract with Ms. Hardnose?
**The Law Says:** No. Only a valid contract can be breached. Frankie's contract was voided, not breached.

# What If?

1. **What If** Ms. Hardnose had let Frankie take the car before he paid for it? Since he was a minor, would he have to pay for the car on the unenforceable (void) contract?

**Answer:** He would either have to return the car or pay for it. Even though the contract was not valid, once Frankie had the car in his possession, the law would not let him be "unjustly enriched," which means it is unlawful to profit from an improper deal.

2. **What If** Frankie Farbush, who is 16, had signed a contract with Ms. Hardnose to buy a winter coat on a freezing cold day? Would that contract be enforceable by either party?

**Answer:** Yes. Certain contracts made by minors are enforceable for important reasons of public policy. Minors can legally contract for the necessities of life such as food, clothing and shelter.

3. **What If** your dad needs 500 apples to make caramel apples for your school's Halloween party? He signs a contract with Sam's Fruit Store to buy the apples for $100. Sam agrees to deliver the apples before the party. The day before the party Sam tells your dad that his truck broke down and he can't deliver the apples in time, but he will drop off the apples the day after Halloween. Your dad knows that will be too late. Dad buys the apples elsewhere for $150. Who is responsible for the extra $50 your dad pays?

**Answer:** Sam, the store owner, is responsible to pay your dad the $50. This is the difference between the contract price and the price your dad finally had to pay. The $50 is known as "difference damages." Even though Sam's failure to deliver the apples on time was not his fault, he will be held to his contractual promise to perform and must pay the consequences if he breaches his promise.

# Activities

1. Work with a partner to write a contract between you. This agreement may be for a service or may involve the sale or trade of an object. Specify who the contracting parties are. What is the time for the performance of the contract? When writing a good contract, it is important to anticipate problems in advance and to try to avoid them. Bargain for your position. Bargaining is a give-and-take process.

2. *Time is of the essence* is a term that is used when referring to a contract. What do you think it means? Why is it important that people perform their end of a bargain when they say they will? Give examples.

3. It is not necessary for money to change hands in a contract. The contracting parties might exchange services. What is most important is that there be an exchange of something of value. In fact, sometimes an agreement *not* to do something can be the basis of a contract. This means that the nonaction of one of the parties must be of value to the other party. For example, sometimes farmers are paid by the government not to plant crops. The value to the government is that crop prices will remain stable and that the land will not be overused.
A classic contract between you and your parents not to do something could be this: If you don't bite your nails for six months, your dad will buy you a watch. Think of other nonaction contracts to negotiate between you and members of your family or friends.

4. **Role Play:** Sports figures, singers, dancers, actors, writers and people in all walks of life enter into contracts. Pretend to represent a favorite celebrity and negotiate, with a tough adversary, for a really good contract. Role-play with one person playing the agent for a favorite celebrity and one person playing the owner of the business (such as a recording company or baseball team).

5. **Role Play:** You are the manager of the Anytown Music Hall. You have contracted with a musical group call The Headlice. On the date of a scheduled appearance, the Lice do not show up. The hall has been sold out of tickets. People in the audience are itchy in anticipation. Get on the telephone and inform the group's agent that they are responsible for your damages. What would you say? What do you think the agent and the Headlice are responsible for (lost ticket sales, rent, stagehands' wages, etc.)? Have the band's agent argue that the band is not responsible because their bus broke down. Discuss what damages caused by the band's breach of contract are too remote (or unreasonable) to be charged to the band. Would it make a difference if the Headlice gave a week's notice of cancellation? What if the audience rioted when they heard the show was cancelled? Who would be responsible?

**"I had every intention of paying for the fudge!"**

After school, Nina Nibbler decides to go to the store to pick up some school supplies. While she is there she buys a loose-leaf notebook, some index cards and a yellow marker. As she passes the candy counter, the smell of freshly popped corn reminds her that she is starting to feel hunger pangs. Quickly looking over the displayed goodies, she sees a luscious wrapped block of chocolate fudge and decides that it looks so delicious she simply can't resist it. As usual, she has selected more items than she planned and has not taken a basket. Because her hands are full, she slips the fudge into her coat pocket, fully intending to pay for it. Before she can get to the checkout counter, she feels the weight of a big hand on her shoulder.

"I saw that fudge go into your pocket, young lady," says a large man, looking directly into her face. "Come with me. You're under arrest for 'larceny from a building.'"

Nina feels her heart constrict and start to beat like a trip hammer. "Oh no!" she protests, "I had every intention of paying for the fudge!"

# What's Your Opinion?

**1.** Can the store detective arrest Nina Nibbler?

**The Law Says:** In most states, yes. A store owner or the agent of the owner can make a citizen's arrest for crimes committed in their presence. Reasonableness is the key. If the attempted arrest is unreasonable, the store may be liable in court for committing a "false arrest."

**2.** Would this be a legitimate arrest even though Nina did not intend to steal the fudge and she had not left the store?

**The Law Says:** In most states, yes. The crime of larceny or attempted larceny is determined by several factors. One necessary element of the crime is the intent to permanently deprive the rightful owner of his possession. In many states it is not absolutely necessary to leave the premises to be found guilty. However, it will be more difficult for the store to prove its case in court since Nina did not actually try to leave the store without paying.

**3.** Is Nina guilty of larceny?

**The Law Says:** No. Larceny requires the intent to steal (to deprive the owner of an object without paying for it). Nina had no such intent. She is not guilty. But she is still in trouble!

**4.** What should you do if you believe you are being arrested or searched unlawfully by a police officer?

**The Law Says:** Clearly state your objections to the actions and then peacefully submit. It is never wise to try to physically resist an arrest performed by a police officer, even if it is an unlawful arrest. If it is unlawful, the products of the search will be excluded as evidence, and you may have a case for filing a suit for false arrest. The only time one should resist an "arrest" is if you feel that someone is using the word *arrest*, as an excuse to assault or kidnap you and is not really a police officer or store detective. But if they are actually legitimate and you resist a real police officer—look out. You're committing a felony and in big-time legal trouble.

**5.** After the police have taken her into custody and made a report, can they continue to keep Nina at the police station?

**The Law Says:** If she is a minor and has committed a nonviolent crime, in most states the police must contact her parents as soon as possible and release her to the custody of her parents until a hearing or trial in juvenile court. If Nina is an adult, the police must release her on "bail," if she can guarantee that she will return to court for trial. (See the Eighth Amendment to the U.S. Constitution.)

# What If?

1. **What If** Nina Nibbler had totally forgotten the fudge and walked out of the store without paying for it, though she had paid for the other merchandise? What would happen if she were arrested? Would she be guilty of larceny then?

**Answer:** No. For Nina's act to be a crime, she must have specifically intended to steal the fudge. If Nina is prosecuted and pleads innocent, a judge or jury would have to decide whether or not she had the intent and whether all other elements of the crime of larceny were also present beyond a reasonable doubt.

2. **What If** Nina had paid for the fudge, but then was seen putting the fudge into her pocket and was stopped by a suspicious store detective? What could she do?

**Answer:** She could produce her sales receipt to prove that she had paid for the fudge. A sales receipt is a legal document! Always wait for your sales receipt, which is your proof of purchase, no matter how small the item may be.

3. **What If** you go to the supermarket, and as you make your way through the aisles, you realize that you are starving and start snacking? You open some packages of sweet treats in your cart to hold off the hunger. The manager comes and accuses you of shoplifting. You protest that you only ate a few small, insignificant items and they were from packages you were going to buy. You insist that they are being ridiculous. Can they really charge you with larceny?

**Answer:** They sure can, though it will not be the strongest case. And the prosecutor may not authorize the charge. The practical lesson here is that you should always avoid even the appearance of taking something that doesn't yet belong to you. Do not eat food or put things in your pocket before you pay for them, even though you intend to purchase them. Appearances do count! Remember, you can sometimes lose a case even though

you are innocent. Even if you are found innocent after a trial, it is not worth going through all the hassle just because you were absent-minded. A man in Michigan was convicted of "retail fraud" (the Michigan shoplifting statute) for eating a few grapes at a grocery store!

4. **What If** you are arrested for shoplifting and before doing anything else, the police officer asks you for your name or identification? Must you respond? Explain the practical and legal reasons why you must identify yourself even if you are innocent.

**Answer:** If you are being accused of a minor crime, if you identify yourself the police officer will often just release you or release you to your parents even if you may be later charged with the crime. If the officer does not know who you are or where you live, he may have no choice but to take you into custody just to find out who you are. However, you need not respond to any other questions.

# What If?

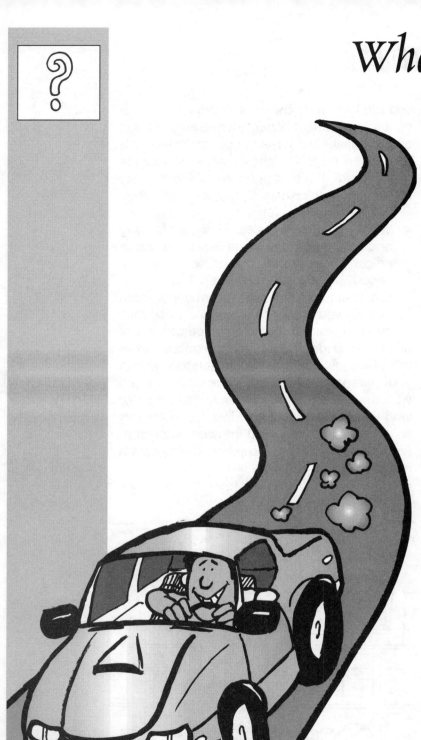

5. **What If** you are arrested for shoplifting and you give your name to the police and they call your parents? If your parents give their permission for you to be questioned, the police must still tell you one more thing before asking you any more questions. Do you know what they must tell you?

**Answer:** The police must tell you what your rights are. These are often called Miranda rights, because the U.S. Supreme Court defined these rights in a case called Miranda vs. Arizona 384 U.S. 436 [1966].) Do you know what the Miranda rights are? You may have seen police warn suspects on television this way:

You have the right to remain silent.
You have the right to an attorney.
If you cannot afford an attorney, one will be appointed for you at public expense.
If you decide to make a statement, anything you say may be used against you in a court of law.

6. **What If** Lester Loophole sees a car at the curb with a key in the ignition. He has taken a course entitled, "Everyday Law for Young Citizens." He remembers that one of the elements of larceny is that the person committing the larceny must intend to permanently deprive the owner of the use and possession of the item taken. Unfortunately, Lester Loophole skipped several of the classes! He decides to take the car for a quick ride. He intends to return the car when he is done and assumes that this is not larceny. Is Lester correct in assuming that this is not larceny?

**Answer:** Yes, he is correct. It is another crime called joy riding. This occurrence is common and in the past seemed to fall between the cracks of the law. Therefore the lawmakers decided to close this loophole and create a law to cover these situations. What is meant by the figure of speech *loophole*?

# Activities

1. The cost to society of petty larceny is much higher than the mere price of the stolen objects. Pretend you are an investigative reporter. Explain in an article how the cost of shoplifting is passed on to the consumer in higher prices. (The owner of a store must make up the losses from the stolen merchandise, by having to pay wages to security people, installing TV monitors and other preventative systems.) Consider also the high costs of administering the criminal justice system (police, courts, judges and jails). Your article may be headed, "Hidden Costs of Crime."

2. Someone steals your homework. It is written on a piece of paper worth only one cent. Would you consider it a fair deal if the punishment to the thief was to pay a fine of one cent? Write your reaction to this. The punishment for larceny may be to pay a fine far greater than the value of the stolen object. Why?
**Answer:** Deterrence and costs noted in number one above. In addition, depriving someone of his or her homework might cause him or her harm.

3. Consider your own personal safety. You are in a store. A person approaches you and claims to be a store detective who suspects you of shoplifting. What should you do or say to protect yourself?
Role-play a scene using the above facts. Consider the outside possibility that the person trying to arrest you may not be who he claims to be and may have other motives for detaining you.
Always ask for identification.
Never leave the store with anyone but a real police officer.
Make sure that the management or police contact your parents as soon as possible—even though it may be embarrassing.

4. Have the students review the first 10 amendments to the Constitution known as the Bill of Rights, and find which one guarantees the rights listed in the Miranda warnings.
**Answer:** The Fifth Amendment.

**"Before too long the party was out of control"**

Moe and Curly's parents were out of town. The boys decided that this was the perfect time to have a big party at their folks' cottage by the lake. Invitations circulated by word of mouth. The news swept the school and on the appointed evening there were more guests than they had expected. As a matter of fact, there were lots of faces that Moe and Curly didn't even recognize!

Some good sports came with chips, soft drinks and assorted munchies. Moe and Curly made sure there was a big supply of beer. The noise began to escalate and before too long the party was out of control, with more than a few people getting seriously drunk. Most of the kids were not even 18.

Close to midnight, a carload of unsteady kids left the house heading toward town. Unfortunately they didn't make it all the way. The car went out of control and struck and seriously injured a pedestrian walking on the sidewalk.

The injured person, Henry Hapless, decided from his wheelchair that he was going to sue for his enormous medical expenses as well as for his pain, suffering and loss of income.

# What's Your Opinion?

1. Who is legally responsible for Henry's injuries?

**The Law Says:** The driver of the car is responsible because 1) he caused Henry's injuries and 2) the driver was negligent. *Negligence* means that the driver neglected to do something he had a duty to do, which was to drive carefully. Moe and Curly are also very likely to be held responsible since they supplied the beer that contributed to the driver's intoxication.

2. What can the pedestrian do if he decides to sue Moe and Curly and finds out that they are minors (under the age of 18) with no money of their own?

**The Law Says:** The pedestrian can file a claim or lawsuit against Moe and Curly's parents. Many states and cities have passed laws explicitly holding parents liable for the irresponsible and unsupervised acts of their minor children. More and more courts are also holding people responsible for damages caused by guests who become drunk at parties in their homes.

3. Did Moe and Curly and their friends commit any crimes in this case? If so, what crimes were committed?

**The Law Says:** Yes. Serving alcohol to minors is a crime. Minors who possess or consume alcohol are committing a crime. Driving while under the influence of alcohol (drunk driving) is a crime. Injuring the pedestrian, Henry Hapless, is criminal negligence, due to the extremely reckless behavior of the drunk driver.

4. How can injuring someone accidentally be a crime if crimes require criminal intent?

**The Law Says:** If one acts in an extremely reckless or dangerous manner which injures other people, the law assumes that one knows that such behavior is likely to cause injury. Therefore, the law says that one who injures another due to recklessness had a "general intent" to cause the injury even though it was an "accident." The law considers reckless behavior more blameworthy than ordinary negligence.

5. Why are the manufacture, sale and use of food, drugs, chemicals, alcoholic beverages, tobacco and firearms more tightly controlled by the government than sales of other substances?

**The Law Says:** Because some substances and products are dangerous if not properly produced and used. The government makes laws to control their use and manufacture to insure the public health and welfare.

# What If?

1. **What If** Moe and Curly did not supply the alcohol at the party but did not stop others from drinking it? Would they and their parents still be responsible for the pedestrian's injury?

**Answer:** It is still very likely that the judge or jury would find Moe and Curly and their parents responsible since Moe and Curly hosted the party and allowed alcohol to be consumed.

2. **What If** we lived in a country where there were no laws at all that regulated the production or manufacture or use of anything? What would be the result?

**Answer:** Chaos would result with serious harm done to many people. There would be many more accidents caused by drunk driving or driving under the influence of drugs. Our environment would become more polluted if manufacturers were not held responsible for the noxious waste products they produced. Foods would be less pure if manufacturers were not held responsible for the inspection of food products and for the prevention of contamination of those food products. More people would die of lung cancer caused by air pollution and cigarettes. More people would be killed and injured by faulty products. There would be no safety outside your home or in your home.

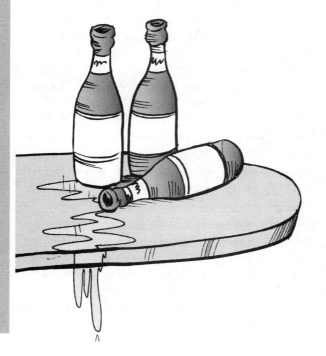

3. **What If** the pedestrian, Henry Hapless, or a passenger in the car had been killed in the accident? Would the driver be guilty of murder?

**Answer:** The driver would be guilty of manslaughter or vehicular homicide. Manslaughter is a homicide (meaning any killing of one person by another) resulting from extreme recklessness. Manslaughter is a crime of "general intent." In this case, the homicide would not be a murder which is a homicide committed intentionally. Murder is often divided into categories. The law considers the worst type of murder (first degree murder) to require premeditation (planning). Second degree murder is intentional but not planned in advance. Killing someone in the heat of an argument is often considered second degree murder.

# Activities

1. Role-play a party at your home. Your good friend arrives and you find out he has been drinking beer and is about to drive home drunk. All of a sudden your friend acts like he is Macho Man. What can you say to him or do to stop him? You and your guests try to work out this problem.

2. Write a list of suggestions for parents, teachers and others in the community that would help reduce drinking and other kinds of substance abuse. Is there a greater problem at school dances and athletic events? Explain your answer. Can you describe a preventative program in your school district or any other you have heard about? How can these programs be improved?

3. With a partner, write a law which you think would regulate alcohol. Include sections on supplying alcohol to minors. Read these laws aloud. Decide who wrote the fairest and most complete law. Could these laws be enforced?

4. Read about alcohol and its effects on the mind and body. Find at least one piece of information that you never knew before (Alcohol is a drug, a 12-ounce can of beer has the same amount of alcohol as a one-ounce glass of whiskey. Drinking enough alcohol in a short time can kill you!). Contribute to a fact-finding session in class. As a good research person, give the title of the book, magazine, pamphlet or newspaper used as your source. Include the copyright date, the page number, the publisher and the city. Why is the copyright date important when one is dealing with information?

**Answer:** Current information is more reliable.

5. What is the minimum legal age in your state for the purchase of alcoholic beverages?

6. Research the national organization called SADD. What is SADD?

**Answer:** SADD stands for: Students Against Destructive Decisions or Students Against

Drunk Driving. It is a student organization designed to increase public awareness of the many hidden pitfalls arising from poor choices and unwise actions.

Their requirements and goals follow:

a. All members are to refrain from using or being involved with people who use illegal controlled substances, such as alcohol, tobacco and marijuana.

b. Members will try to make those in their community aware of the dangers of such activities and encourage them to lead a better life-style, not by being judgmental, but by showing support and kindness.

c. Whenever students are faced with a situation which may endanger themselves in any way, they are encouraged not to be afraid or ashamed to call an adult or friend to give them a ride or other necessary assistance.

SADD was formed by a high school coach from Wayland, Massachusetts, in 1981, after the tragic loss of two well-known students to an alcohol-related automobile accident. The original name was an acronym for Students Against Drunk Driving. Over the years, it has had many different names such as Student Athletes Detest Drugs and others of a similar nature. Eventually it was decided that Students Against Destructive Decisions was the most appropriate and encompassed all the things that could and would get a person into trouble.

# Activities

7. Research the national organization called Mothers Against Drunk Driving, or MADD.
**Answer:** MADD is an organization that lobbies for more effective legislation against drunk driving and urges strong penalties. They aim to increase public awareness and to take action. They conduct research and compile statistics. Look up the Mothers Against Drunk Driving web site: http://madd.org/ or write to MADD, P.O. Box 541688, Dallas, TX 75354-1688 or phone: 800-GET-MADD.

8. Define *controlled substance*.
**Answer:** A controlled substance is any material or product whose manufacture, sale and/or use is controlled or regulated by laws (insecticides, prescription drugs, illegal drugs, tobacco, guns, alcoholic beverages, fuels, chemicals). Brainstorm a list of controlled substances on a chart or on the board.

9. If some substances are so dangerous, why are they allowed to be used at all?
**Answer:** Because they are also beneficial (for example: gasoline and insecticides). Some substances, such as heroin and the insecticide DDT are so dangerous or provide so little benefit that the law makes them completely illegal. What do you think are the dangers and benefits of controlled substances you've listed? Are there any benefits to tobacco or alcohol? Who benefits from the manufacture and sale of those substances?

Construct a chart which illustrates controlled substances and their dangers and benefits. Below are some possible answers.

1. Foods are inspected to insure the purity of what we eat and to prevent food poisoning.
2. Prescription drugs are regulated to guarantee purity and to avoid misuse or abuse.
3. Production and sale of chemicals are regulated to control waste produced when they are manufactured and to insure that chemicals are not improperly used.
4. Fuels such as coal and gasoline are inspected for purity to minimize the toxic gases that result from their combustion. Bad fuels can damage the machines that burn them. Gasoline is explosive if improperly used.
5. Alcoholic beverages are regulated to insure that they are properly produced. Improperly made or impure alcohol can cause blindness, convulsions and death. Alcohol sales are regulated to avoid use by minors and abuse by adults.
6. Firearms are regulated so that extremely dangerous weapons such as machine guns do not get into the hands of criminals.
7. Insecticides must be used only in approved ways in order to prevent harm to humans and animals. Insecticides are tested and regulated to minimize dangerous and unpredictable side effects on the environment.
8. Hazardous building products such as asbestos, solvents and glue are regulated to reduce exposure of workers and consumers. A prime example of this is the strict regulation on removal of asbestos which was used widely in schools and offices as insulation and can cause lung cancer if it becomes airborne and inhaled.

# Robbery/Larceny from a Person
# Case of the Reluctant Donation

Betsy Bystander was minding her own business in the hall of Anytown High when she saw Stella Strongarm, one of the must threatening students in the school. Stella was always trouble. Betsy tried her best to become part of the wall and blend in with the background, but it didn't work. She had once read something about how not to look like a victim, but she couldn't remember the advice, and Stella was coming toward her like a steamroller.

"Hey, Baby Face, I need a dollar and I need it right now, so just hand one over if you know what's good for you!" Betsy backed away from the sneering Stella. "If I give you a dollar, I won't have enough for lunch!" she pleaded.

"That's not my problem. Just hand it over, or else!"

Betsy, feeling as if she had no choice, dug down into her jacket pocket, withdrew the dollar, and gave it to the looming Stella, who walked away laughing.

**"Hand it over if you know what's good for you!"**

# What's Your Opinion?

1. Was Stella's behavior criminal? If so, what crime was committed?

**The Law Says:** Yes. Stella committed a robbery. Robbery is also known as "larceny from a person." *Robbery* means "taking property from a person by force or fear." Although there was no overt threat of force, it was clear from Stella's manner and words when she said, "If you know what's good for you" and "hand it over, or else!"

2. Why is "shoplifting" a misdemeanor while "larceny from a person" (robbery) is a felony? (Remember, a felony is a more serious crime than a misdemeanor. A felony is punishable by imprisonment for longer than a year. A misdemeanor is a less serious crime and may be punishable by imprisonment for less than a year.)

**The Law Says:** Robbery involves taking money or valuables directly from a person with violence or threats of violence. The law considers crimes of violence against people more serious than crimes against property.

# What If?

1. **What If** Stella Strongarm had said, "Lend me a dollar," instead of "Give me a dollar," would that still be a crime?

**Answer:** This is a closer question, which would depend upon whether Stella had intended to return the money or whether her behavior was merely a dishonest strategy.

2. **What If** Stella Strongarm sees that her neighbor is out mowing the lawn. Stella quickly goes around to the rear of her neighbor's house, quietly opens the back screen door and slips into the empty kitchen. In a flash, she grabs a $5 bill off the kitchen table and sneaks out quickly! Is this crime a felony or a misdemeanor? Why?

**Answer:** In most states this crime would be considered the felony of breaking and entering. The law considers it to be a more serious crime when one unlawfully enters a building to commit a larceny, even though a small amount of money may be involved. Breaking and entering does not literally mean the felon must break anything. Slipping in through a window or unlocked door can still be considered breaking and entering.

3. Before a trial, when a defendant is charged, he or she is formally told what the penalties might be if he or she is found guilty of that crime. If it is a jury trial, the jury does not hear what potential penalties might be. Why do you think this is so?

**Answer:** To ensure that they will decide only on the issue of whether the defendant is innocent or guilty, and not to alter their verdict out of feelings that the penalty might be too severe for the crime.

# Activity: Mock Trial Role Play

## The People vs. Stella Strongarm

Stella is over 18 and is therefore being tried as an adult in front of a jury. Below are complete instructions on how to structure a role play and mock trial.

### To the Teacher

Duplicate pages 45-47 (on both sides of the paper) as a handout for each student. With partners, as a class, read orally and carefully: "How a Trial Is Structured."

### Appoint

1. a prosecuting attorney to represent the State and Betsy Bystander (the victim)
2. a defense attorney to represent Stella Strongarm (the accused)
3. a judge (perhaps the teacher)
4. a bailiff
5. a court recorder
6. a student to act the part of Stella Strongarm (the defendant)
7. one student to act the part of Betsy Bystander (the complaining witness)
8. members of the jury pool
9. several witnesses: some friendly to Stella some friendly to Betsy

Hand out cue cards (pages 48-51) to the bailiff, judge, prosecutor, defense attorney and court recorder. Hand out juror cue cards (pages 52-53) to prospective jurors as role-play clues. Most potential jurors should receive a card that says: "You are not biased." After choosing the jury, hand out witness cue cards (page 51) to the witnesses. Feel free to have students make up their own stories as witnesses or biases as jurors.

# How a Trial Is Structured

**Pre-Trial Hearing (Arraignment):** Long before the trial, the accused is told what the charges will be and what the possible penalties are so he or she can prepare a defense.

**The Trial:** At the beginning of the trial, when the judge enters, the bailiff loudly says, "All rise. The District Court for the County of ( ) is now in session. The Honorable Judge (judge's last name) presiding." After the judge enters and is seated say, "Please be seated."

**Seating the Jury:** The two attorneys will pick a jury (of 6 or 12) from members of the class. All prospective jurors will be asked questions to make sure they are qualified and not biased. This process is called "voir dire" (pronounced "vwor deer") which means "to speak the truth." Any juror who appears to be biased or unable to serve for some other reason will be eliminated at the discretion of the judge, at the request of either attorney.

If jurors are chosen from the jury pool, they must try to set aside their biases. If a juror is eliminated for bias, a new juror is chosen from the pool until all sides agree that the jury is acceptable.

Prospective jurors may not lie. Attorneys cannot merely ask: "Do you have any biases?" but must ask specific questions such as: "Does any juror know the Defendant, the Plaintiff or their families?" The judge may also "voir dire" jurors and eliminate any juror who is biased or is unable to render a fair and impartial verdict or is unable to serve for any reason.

The judge swears in the jury saying, "Do you solemnly swear that you will render a fair and impartial verdict in this case to the best of your ability?"

**The Defendant Is Charged:** After the jury is selected, at the beginning of the trial, the judge will read the prosecution's charges against the defendant. "Defendant, you are charged with the crime of larceny from a person, also known as unarmed robbery. If convicted, you will face a sentence of up to five years in jail and a fine up to $10,000. How do you plead?"

The defendant says, "Not Guilty, Your Honor."

In a real trial, the jury would not be present when the potential penalties are read.

**Opening Statements:** After a jury is chosen, the prosecutor and defense attorney each make opening statements to support their cases. Witnesses testify after being sworn in by the bailiff. The bailiff administers the oath to witnesses saying, "Please raise your right hand. Do you solemnly swear to tell the truth, the whole truth and nothing but the truth?"

The prosecutor starts first because the prosecution has the burden of proving the guilt of the defendant.

**Examination and Cross-Examination:** The prosecutor calls Betsy Bystander and her witnesses individually to the stand for direct examination. After each witness for the prosecution is examined, the defense attorney cross-examines them in turn. Any evidence is introduced and marked as exhibits (such as the money Stella Strongarm took or, if Betsy was threatened with a weapon, the weapon). After all the witnesses for the prosecution are examined and cross-examined, the prosecution rests. (Usually this is done by telling the judge that she or he has no more witnesses to call.)

Then the defense attorney calls witnesses for the defense, whose testimony may help Stella prove her innocence. At this time, Stella may testify on her own behalf. After each witness has given his or her testimony, the prosecutor then cross-examines that witness.

When the defense finishes its case, the defense "rests."

# How a Trial Is Structured

Although criminal defendants may not be forced to testify, if they do decide to testify at trial, they must also submit to cross-examination by the prosecutor.

Throughout the trial, each attorney may object, or try to have struck down, questions the opposing attorney asks a witness, as they are asked and before the witness answers. The judge rules, or decides on the objections. If the judge agrees with the objection, he or she says, "Objection sustained. Witness, do not answer that question because it is improper." If the judge disagrees with the objection, he or she will say, "Objection overruled. The witness may answer the question."

If an attorney, witness or bystander is rude or fails to obey the judge's order, the judge would say, "You are in contempt of court." The judge may assess a fine and/or have the person in contempt removed from the courtroom by the bailiff!

**Closing Arguments:** After the prosecution and the defense rest their cases, they are allowed to make closing arguments to the jury. This is the last chance for each attorney to try to convince the jury to decide in favor of his or her client.

# How a Trial Is Structured

**Judge's Instructions to the Jury:** After both sides rest and make closing arguments, the judge addresses the jury. She or he repeats the charge against the defendant and tells the jury that they must weigh the evidence in order to decide whether it meets the legal standard required to convict. In a criminal case the prosecutor must have proved the guilt of the defendant beyond a reasonable doubt.

**Jury Deliberations:** The jury deliberates in private. The jury picks a foreperson who will direct discussion and who will tell the court when they have reached a decision and what that decision is. The jury verdict in a criminal trial must be unanimous.

**Verdict:** After the jury reaches a decision, the foreperson tells the bailiff and the jury is brought back into court. The judge asks if they have reached a decision and, if so, who speaks for the jury? The foreperson identifies him- or herself as the foreperson.

Then the judge asks what the jury's verdict is. The foreperson tells the court whether they have decided the defendant is guilty or not guilty. The judge will ask if this was their unanimous decision. The foreperson must say "yes."

If the jury can't agree to convict or acquit, a mistrial is declared, which means the trial will have to be held again with a new jury. (A jury which can't agree on a verdict is known as a hung jury.)

**Sentence:** If the jury convicts the defendant, the judge pronounces the sentence, or punishment. The sentence is decided upon by taking into account the circumstances of the crime, standard sentencing guidelines (which are proposed to make sentencing fair and uniform), the prosecutor's recommendation and the judge's experience. The sentence may include restitution (a fine levied to pay back the plaintiff for his or her loss), counseling, community service, probation and in the case of serious crimes and repeat offenders: jail.

# Cue Cards

**CUE: Judge: You are in charge of the trial.**

At the beginning of the trial, you swear in the jury saying, "Do you solemnly swear that you will render a fair and impartial verdict in this case to the best of your ability?"

After the jury is selected, at the beginning of the trial, you read the prosecution's charges against the defendant: "Defendant, you are charged with the crime of larceny from a person, also known as unarmed robbery. If convicted, you will face a sentence of up to five years in jail and a fine up to $10,000. How do you plead?" The defendant will then plead guilty or not guilty. In a real trial, the jury does not hear the possible penalties.

The judge calls the defense attorney "Counsel" or "Counselor" and the prosecutor, "Mr. or Ms. Prosecutor."

During the trial, if the prosecutor or defense attorney do not feel that a question to a witness is appropriate (see Objection Cue Card on page 51), they can object before the witness answers. If the judge agrees with the objections she or he says, "Objection sustained. Witness, do not answer that question because it is improper." If the judge disagrees with the objection, she or he will say: "Objection overruled. The witness may answer the question."

If an attorney, witness or bystander is rude or fails to obey a judge's order, you would say, "You are in contempt of court." You may assess a fine and/or have the person in contempt removed from the courtroom by the bailiff.

After both attorneys have rested their case and made their closing statements, it is your responsibility to instruct the jury as to how they are to consider the evidence. You will say, "Members of the jury, the Defendant, Stella Strongarm, is charged with unarmed robbery also known as larceny from a person. Remember, she is innocent until proven guilty. If after listening to all of the testimony you believe beyond a reasonable doubt that Stella Strongarm is guilty of the crime of larceny from a person, you must find her guilty. If you have any reasonable doubt about her intent to permanently deprive Betsy Bystander of her money by force or fear, or if you are not convinced that it was indeed the defendant who took the money, you must find the defendant not guilty. You may decide that some evidence or testimony is more reliable than other testimony. To be guilty, it must be proven beyond a reasonable doubt that Stella forced Betsy Bystander to give Stella money against Betsy's will.

If the defendant does not testify, add this jury instruction: "In this country, the defendant has the right not to testify at trial. Because the defendant has chosen not to testify at trial, you must not consider that as any evidence of guilt."

Then you say to the jury, "You may now deliberate."

When the jury returns from their deliberation, you ask, "Who speaks for the jury?" The foreperson will identify him- or herself. You then ask, "What is your verdict?" The foreperson will announce the verdict. You ask if the verdict is unanimous, and the foreperson must say that it is.

For example, "Stella Strongarm, you have been found guilty of unarmed robbery. You are hereby sentenced to pay a fine and costs of $500 and to do 100 hours of community service at a local charity, which will be monitored by your probation officer."

If the verdict is "guilty," the judge must pronounce sentence upon the defendant.

If the verdict is "not guilty," the judge announces that the defendant has been acquitted and is free to go.

The judge then thanks the jury for their service and says, "Court is now adjourned."

# Cue Cards

**CUE: The Bailiff:** the bailiff is usually a police officer who helps keep order in the court.

At the beginning of the trial, when the judge enters, the bailiff loudly says, "All rise. The District Court for the County of ( ) is now in session. The Honorable Judge (judge's last name) presiding." After the judge enters and is seated say, "Please be seated."

When testimony is taken, the bailiff administers the oath to witnesses saying, "Please raise your right hand. Do you solemnly swear to tell the truth, the whole truth and nothing but the truth?"

If the judge determines that someone is unruly or in contempt of court, the bailiff will escort him or her out of the courtroom.

**CUE: The Court Recorder:** The court recorder makes an exact transcript of every word spoken during the proceedings on a stenotype machine.

In this case, an approximation of the proceedings will be fine or a tape recorder or even a videotape may be used. The court recorder may be asked to clarify testimony when parties disagree about what has been testified to.

**CUE: Betsy Bystander: You are the plaintiff.**

Stella made you give her a dollar. You felt you had no choice or Stella would hurt you. You are sure it was Stella and not someone else.

**CUE: Stella Strongarm: You are the defendant.**

You will plead "not guilty" when the judge charges you at the beginning of the trial. You proclaim your innocence. You have a choice as to whether you will testify in your defense or not ("take the Fifth"). However, if you decide to testify, you must submit to cross-examination by the prosecutor. You might claim that you were only asking to borrow the money. Or maybe Betsy has you mixed up with someone else.

# Cue Cards

**CUE: Prosecuting Attorney: You are the attorney for the "people." It is your responsibility to persuade the judge and/or jury that the defendant is responsible for committing a crime and should be punished.**

The prosecution has the burden of proof. In other words, you are responsible for finding and bringing together the evidence (witness' testimony, the stolen item or any weapons involved).

The prosecutor must prove all of the elements of the crime beyond a reasonable doubt. They are 1) Stella threatened Betsy into giving her money, 2) Betsy was reasonably fearful for her safety if she did not give Betsy money, 3) It was Stella and no one else who committed the robbery.

You will make an "opening statement" to the jury telling them what you intend to prove and why Stella is guilty.

You must call witnesses to testify. You must have the witnesses tell the facts in order to prove the case. You must decide what are the right questions to ask the witnesses in order to bring out the facts. An example of a necessary fact: Betsy must identify Stella as the robber. After calling all the witnesses, the prosecution rests.

After the defense attorney calls and examines witnesses, you cross-examine them. In your questioning, you will try to make it clear to the judge and jury that there are aspects of their testimony which would make it unreliable or less believable. For example, you may try to show that they are biased in favor of the defendant and thus be interpreting the incident in a way favorable to her. Or you may cast doubt on whether they saw or remember the incident clearly (perhaps by asking questions about whether they remember events before and after the Strongarm incident). After the cross-examination you will rest your case.

After both sides have rested, the prosecution will make a closing argument to the jury. The closing argument should sum up the evidence and persuade the jury that it is enough to convict the defendant of the crime.

**CUE: Defense Attorney: You try to show that no crime took place, or that there were mitigating circumstances which would partially exonerate your client.**

After the prosecutor makes an opening statement, the defense attorney makes an opening statement telling the jury why Stella is innocent.

The defense attorney "cross-examines" the prosecutor's witnesses to see if there are weaknesses in what they say. You will ask them questions which will cast doubt on the reliability of their testimony. Perhaps Stella Strongarm was just joking or Betsy really wanted to give Stella the money but was afraid to tell her mom, or perhaps someone who looked like Stella Strongarm robbed Betsy Bystander. You may try to show that they are biased in favor of the plaintiff and thus be interpreting the incident in a way favorable to her. Or you may cast doubt on whether they saw or remember the incident clearly (perhaps by asking questions about whether they remember events before and after the Strongarm incident).

After the prosecuting attorney "rests," it is your turn to call defense witnesses. After the prosecutor cross-examines your witnesses, you will rest your case. Then you will make a closing argument to the jury.

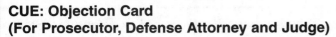

**CUE: Objection Card**
**(For Prosecutor, Defense Attorney and Judge)**

While your opposing counsel is questioning witnesses, you may "object" if you think that a question is improper for one or more of the following reasons by saying, "Your Honor, I object to the question because it is (pick one or more) . . . ."

1. Irrelevant (not related to proving the case)

2. Asking for hearsay (asks for an answer not in the direct knowledge of the witness)

3. Leading (it gives the witness a hint by giving the answer within the question. Leading questions are acceptable on cross examination, but not on direct examination. (Attorneys directly examine their own "friendly" witnesses and cross-examine the opposition's "unfriendly" witnesses.) An example of a leading question would be if the prosecutor asked a defense witness on cross-examination, "You saw Stella ask Betsy for money, didn't you?"

The judge will either sustain or dismiss your objection. If the objection is sustained, the witness will not have to answer the question. If the objection is overruled, the witness has to answer.

**CUE: Witness for the Defense:** You think that you saw Stella at the movies at the time the crime supposedly occurred. You aren't completely sure since it was dark in the theater. But you are a friend of Stella's and would like to help her out. However, you are not willing to lie.

**CUE: Witness for the Prosecution:** You were standing across the hall when Betsy gave Stella the money. You aren't friends with either girl. You couldn't hear what happened, but you think Betsy looked scared and Stella looked threatening. You definitely saw Betsy give the money to Stella.

**CUE: Police Officer:** You investigated the crime after Betsy reported it to her mother and her mother called you. You spoke to both girls. Most of what you have to tell is hearsay and is not admissible as evidence.

**CUE: A Nearby Teacher:** You saw Betsy give Stella the money. You could see that Stella did not look happy, but you could not hear exactly what was said. You also know that Stella is always getting in trouble, although that is not relevant here unless she has been caught "shaking down" other students in the past.

**CUE: A Student:** You were next to Betsy when Stella approached her. You think Stella was threatening Betsy for the money. You once got into a fight with Stella about a loan, but you don't think that will affect your truthfulness.

# Juror Cue Cards

You may be biased in favor of the prosecution because:
You believe that if Stella is in court, she must be guilty.

You may be biased in favor of the defendant, Stella Strongarm, because:
You were once unfairly convicted of shoplifting.

You may be biased in favor of the prosecution because:
You don't like Stella's looks.

You may be biased in favor of the defendant, Stella Strongarm, because:
You work for Stella's father.

You may be biased in favor of the prosecution because:
You were once mugged on the street.

You may be biased in favor of the defendant, Stella Strongarm, because:
You were once sued by Betsy Bystander's family.

You may be biased in favor of the prosecution because:
You are a police officer.

You may be biased in favor of the defendant, Stella Strongarm, because:
You are a criminal defense lawyer.

You may be biased in favor of the prosecution because:
You are a friend of Betsy's family.

You may be biased in favor of the defendant, Stella Strongarm, because:
You are a friend of the defense lawyer.

You may be biased in favor of the prosecution because:
You read a story in the newspaper about this case that sounded like Stella was guilty.

You may be biased in favor of the defendant, Stella Strongarm, because:
You believe that Betsy looks like a liar.

You cannot sit on the jury because your mother is going to the hospital for an operation and you have to be with her. You should ask to be excused.

You cannot sit on the jury because you had a back injury, and you cannot sit for long periods.

You cannot sit on the jury because you are taking medicine that makes you sleepy.

52

# Juror Cue Cards

| | |
|---|---|
| You are not biased for or against either side. | You are not biased for or against either side. |
| You are not biased for or against either side. | You are not biased for or against either side. |
| You are not biased for or against either side. | You are not biased for or against either side. |
| You are not biased for or against either side. | You are not biased for or against either side. |
| You are not biased for or against either side. | You are not biased for or against either side. |
| You are not biased for or against either side. | You are not biased for or against either side. |
| You are not biased for or against either side. | You are not biased for or against either side. |
| You are not biased for or against either side. | You are not biased for or against either side. |

# Children and Parents' Rights and Responsibilities
# Case of the Forged Working Papers

Gracie Gogetter was 15. She decided to answer an ad in a local newspaper and get a newspaper route. She went to the local office of the *Daily Bugle* and applied. She was told that because she was under 18 she would need to have a work permit signed by her parents. Gracie was excited. She would easily be able to make $20 a week delivering papers.

Because she was in a hurry, Gracie did not take the work permit all the way home. Instead of having her mother or father sign it, Gracie signed it herself with her mother's name.

Gracie took the permit back to the newspaper office. They hardly looked at the signature and assigned Gracie a paper route on the spot. She began delivering the paper conscientiously after school that week.

After a few weeks of delivering the newspaper, Gracie's mom noticed that she had much more money than she received for her allowance.

"I'm sorry, Gracie," her mother replied. "Your grades in school are poor enough as it is. I don't want you using homework time delivering papers. And besides that, I'm going to complain to the newspaper because they let you work without my permission!"

Mrs. Gogetter called the *Daily Bugle* office. After a brief conversation, she put down the phone, turned and angrily gave Gracie a hard slap. Furthermore, her mother took away all Gracie's earnings and put them in a bank account maintained for Gracie's college education.

**"Gracie's mom took away all of her earnings."**

# What's Your Opinion?

1. Can Gracie's mother take away money that Gracie earned from the paper route?

**The Law Says:** Yes. Until you reach the age of majority (legal adulthood) which is 18 in most states, parents have the right to control your finances, even money you have earned yourself. However, parents also have the legal responsibility to financially support their children as well, supplying all their basic needs for food, shelter, clothing and medical care.

2. Can Gracie's mother slap her or ground her for such a minor offense?

**The Law Says:** Yes. Parents have a right to use a "reasonable" amount of force or corporal punishment to discipline their children and regulate their behavior.

3. Was the station manager of the *Daily Bugle* guilty of breaking the law?

**The Law Says:** No, not unless he had a reason to know that Mrs. Gogetter's signature was forged. If he knew it was a forgery, he would be guilty of violation of the state's labor laws.

# What If?

1. **What If** Gracie's mother had given her permission to work? Could she still have taken Gracie's earnings?

**Answer:** Yes. Since Gracie's parents have the responsibility of supporting her until she reaches the age of majority (18), they are also entitled to control any wages she makes until that time.

2. **What If** Gracie's mother told Gracie's dad and he was so furious that he whipped her with his belt until she had bruises all over her body? Is that a crime?

**Answer:** Yes. Even parents cannot inflict excessive discipline on their children. Serious beatings that raise welts or make bruises or which are frequent or severe, cross into the area of "child abuse."

3. **What If** Gracie's parents were guilty of discipline which was too extreme? What could Gracie do?

**Answer:** Gracie could tell her school teacher, counselor, the police or call the state agency responsible for the protection of children. These people can and will help. They are required by law to assist and protect children in danger. No one deserves abusive of treatment.

# Activities

1. Since the rules which govern child labor vary from state to state, write to your State Labor Department to find out what you would need to do in order to be employed. What do you think the regulations should include?

2. To understand the need for child labor laws, research the history of the factory system in this country and in England. During the Industrial Revolution in the eighteenth, nineteenth and early twentieth centuries, children as young as five years old worked in coal mines, textile mills, tobacco factories and many other industries. These children, who were not given an education, were virtual captives of an economic system which crowded them into dangerous, unsanitary factories and worked them 10 to 16 hours a day.

   How could it happen that the laws in England and then in America permitted this to take place and justified it as well? What kinds of attitudes existed in our country before 1938 when the Wages and Hours Act was finally passed? It was this act that is now the basic child labor law for the United States. Prepare a group report on this gruesome and shameful chapter in history. Research child labor abuses existing today in this country and other parts of the world.

3. You are a state legislator. Write a law and/or argue for a law to regulate child labor. Specify the kinds of work children under 18 can or cannot do. Include limits on hours they can work, weights they can lift and specific jobs that are too dangerous, dirty or otherwise unfit. Also include a provision for minimum wages. How would you make your laws enforceable? What kinds of penalties would you impose on employers who violated your laws?

**Role Play:** "Congress is now in session." Take versions of the laws written above and have the class debate them as if each student was a legislator from a different area. Some legislators should represent farm areas where family farms depend on their children to help. Some legislators should represent industrial areas where teenagers are seen as a good source of low-wage workers. Have a representative from OSHA (Occupational Safety and Health Administration) present statistics about how many teenagers are injured or killed on the job each year. Make sure one or two legislators claim that their own teenagers' academic success has faltered because they are too tired from their after-school jobs to study properly. Have some discuss lowering the minimum wage for people under 18. Have one student act as a lobbyist for newspapers who depend on young paper carriers. Create compromise legislation until one version finally passes by a majority vote.

# Divorce/Child Custody
## Case of the Poor Divorced Parent

Max and Sara Stalwart were married and had two children: Junior, nine, and Missy, 12. Max was a jazz musician and Sara was a nurse. Max worked at different "gigs" all over the country, and Sara worked at a nearby hospital.

Max and Sara weren't getting along too well. Max was so often away from home that Sara felt he wasn't able to do his share in the marriage. Max was, however, trying hard to make a living as a musician, which was his only skill.

Unable to reconcile their differences, Sara filed for a divorce in the state court. Max was sad but didn't contest the divorce. Sara asked the court for custody of Junior and Missy. Max agreed. Junior thought he'd rather travel around with his dad than live with his mom, but no one asked about his preference.

On the day of the court hearing, the judge granted the divorce and awarded the custody of Junior and Missy to their mom. The judge ordered Max to give Sara money each month for child support. The amount of support was based on Max and Sara's incomes with a formula determined by the state. The judge gave Max the right to visit the children or have them visit him once a week and on some holidays.

Unfortunately, Max often failed to give Sara the money for child support. Sara still worked at the hospital, but without money from Max, it was hard to make ends meet.

# What's Your Opinion?

1. Should the judge ask the children which parent they would prefer to live with? Should the children's preferences be the determining factor for the court to use when deciding custody?

**The Law Says:** If the parents have already decided between them which parent will get custody of the children, the courts will likely honor the parents' decision. If the parents cannot decide themselves and are battling over custody of the children, some judges will ask the children what their preferences are, especially if the children are older. In contested cases, the final decision will be made by the judge.

2. What standards or guidelines should a judge use when deciding which parent should get custody of the children?

**The Law Says:** The law is very clear that the judge must decide based upon "the best interest of the child." This would include which parent can provide the most stable environment, which situation would cause the least disruption on the lives of the children and which parent can take the best care of the children. However, the judge should not consider which parent makes the most money when making the decision.

3. Isn't it possible that the parents could share custody even though the parents are not living together after the divorce?

**The Law Says:** Yes, it is possible that the children could alternate for more or less equal periods of time between the parents. Courts are increasingly accepting this arrangement known legally as "joint custody." Usually the children go back and forth between the parents' homes, but sometimes the children stay in one home and the parents alternate living there.

4. Is there anywhere Sara's family can seek assistance since they can't make ends meet on her salary alone?

**The Law Says:** Yes. If there is a need for help, all states have assistance programs called Aid to Families with Dependent Children (AFDC or ADC). To qualify, there are certain income guidelines and a certain amount of paperwork, but local welfare or social service officials can often help speed up the process especially in emergencies.

5. Will the government help Sara collect child support from Max? How?

**The Law Says:** Yes. All states have mechanisms for enforcing support orders when the "noncustodial" parent fails to pay. In many states an agency called the Friend of the Court or a similar agency will automatically begin collection procedures against the non-paying parent. However, it is always helpful for the custodial parent (Sara, in this case) to call that agency and make sure they know about the problem and begin to act. Although the children live with their mother, the father is equally responsible under the law for the support of his children until they reach 18 years of age.

# What If?

1. **What If** Max loses his job?  Is he still responsible for child support?

**Answer:** Yes.  Although losing a job is serious, so is the responsibility for child support. Courts will sometimes reduce the amount of monthly support payments if a parent loses a job or takes a job at a lower salary.  But the court will not go below a certain minimum amount.  The court may also allow the parent to delay support payments until he gets a new job, but he must ultimately pay the "arrearage" (the amount that he falls behind).

2. **What If** Sara remarries?  Is Max still responsible for child support, even if Sara's new husband is very rich?

**Answer:** Yes.  Unless Sara's new husband legally adopts Junior and Missy and assumes responsibility for their support, Max is still responsible.  The new husband could only adopt the children if Max agrees to the adoption (unless Max abandons the children and the court terminates his rights).

3. **What If** your parents are divorced and your noncustodial parent comes to pick you up unexpectedly from home or school?  You suspect that your custodial parent has not consented to this visit and you feel uncomfortable.  What should you do?

**Answer:** If you have any doubts about going with your parent at that time, try to inform your custodial parent.  If you are in school, tell your teacher or principal and ask him or her to contact your other parent.  Do not leave before permission is granted and everyone is sure the plan is OK.

# Activities

1. **What About Grandparents?** Currently, all 50 states allow courts to give grandparents the right to visit with their grandchildren if the parents divorce. The state of Washington tried to go even further. Their legislature passed a law allowing ANYONE to petition the court for visitation of children in a divorce if the court found it to be in the "best interest of the child." The Supreme Court of Washington ruled that the law was unconstitutional because it violated a parent's constitutional rights to raise children without state interference.

The case was argued January 12, 2000, before the U.S. Supreme Court. The suit, Troxel v. Granville, No. 99-138, was originally filed by two grandparents who were trying to get legal visitation rights after their son died and their daughter-in-law remarried and limited visits with their grandchildren.

The mother argued that parents should have an absolute right to determine who gets the right to visit with their child. The grandparents argued that anyone who has a legitimate relationship with a child should be allowed to visit if the court decides it is in the child's best interest.

Many outside groups have filed Amicus briefs (also know as "friend of the court" briefs). A brief tries to persuade the court to adopt its interpretation of the law. Amicus briefs are filed in a case by persons or organizations which may not have legal standing in that particular suit but which have an interest in the law created by the final decision in the case. In this case, the court allowed briefs from 12 state attorney generals, the AARP (representing grandparents), the Legal Services of Southeastern Michigan (representing poor parents) and several conservative Christian groups (representing the traditional view of parents' rights).

The implications of this case are enormous. Not only does this decision potentially affect all family law (law which regulates marriage, divorce and adoption) but the grandparents' brief warns that "to accept the Washington Supreme Court's notion of parental control over ideas to which children should be exposed would have 'revolutionary implications' for parental veto power over the curriculum in public schools." (*New York Times,* p A11, Jan. 4, 2000)

Have the students brainstorm and develop a list of organizations which would be interested in filing Friend of the Court briefs. (Hint: they include religious groups, noncustodial parents' organizations, legal services representing poor people and grandparent groups among others.) Have each select a viewpoint, write a short position paper and present it to the class. Have the class guess the probable outcome of the case, given the current state of law at this time. Then research the final decision in Troxell vs. Granville and see whether your predictions are right or wrong.

# Activities

2. **Taking Care of Baby:** Having children is a responsibility for the parents which involves a lifetime commitment of love and caring. The human baby is the most helpless and dependent of all the mammals. This relationship of child dependency and parental responsibility is cleverly demonstrated by a school lesson which was devised to emphasize the rigors of parenting. We will call it The Coddling of Baby Egg. Each student will care for a raw egg as if it were an infant, for one week. The teacher will sign each egg to guarantee there will be no substitutions in case of mishaps or "child" abuse. The students must make a crib or carrier for the egg and take it with them everywhere. The "infants" must be cared for 24 hours a day.

As in real life, if the "parent" absolutely can't take the "infant" with him or her, then a dependable "egg-sitter" must be found who will take the chore seriously. "Baby" may be dressed and made to look like the real thing. No fair if you hard-boil the "Baby." The teacher will break the eggs at the end of the week to check. During the project keep a journal of your experiences. After the project, write a reflective paper on the fragility, the inconvenience and the constant burden of care Baby Egg required. What can you conclude from this about authentic child care?

3. There is a series of books, *Amber Brown* by Paula Danziger, which deals with the issues of divorce for elementary age children. Call your local library to see what books they have on this topic, or talk to a school counselor to see if he or she has other resources to recommend. Online, you might want to check the Internet Public Library http://www.ipl.org or the American Library Association web site, http://www.ala.org/. Are any of these books written by kids who have gone through a divorce themselves?

4. List on the chalkboard reasons for the following: How is a marriage a legal contract?

**Answer:** Contracts require that the parties exchange one thing of value for another. In marriage, the parties exchange vows (promises). They promise to love, honor and cherish each other. Do you think that these promises are valuable enough to form the basis of a contract?

5. Marriage is different from any other contract. Can you list the ways that it is different?

**Answer:** 1) It requires a license issued by the state before the parties can enter into it. Most other contracts do not require state approval or licenses. 2) If the parties want to end a marriage contract, the state court must supervise the divorce. Other contracts can be ended by mutual consent of the parties, without government approval.

6. Some people believe that once a couple marries, they should not be allowed to divorce. What do you think?

# Vandalism/Malicious Destruction of Property
## Case of the Graffiti Artist

**Overcome with inspiration, she spray painted the school wall.**

Rebecca Rembrandt and Sammy Cezanne, two aspiring neighborhood artists, wanted to create a chalk masterpiece on Sammy's driveway. With permission from Sammy's mom, they were soon hard at work with plenty of chalk, transforming their big concrete "canvas" into a work of art.

After a little while, Rebecca got bored with the driveway and decided to move on to bigger and better things. She found a can of red spray paint and headed to the school across the street. Overcome with inspiration, she spray painted the school with the words *So many walls, So little time.*

Just as she was finishing, a police car pulled up. The police detained Rembrandt and told her she was under arrest for "malicious destruction of property." "But I didn't destroy anything!" she protested. "And if this is a crime,

then I'm not the only one who is a criminal. Look what Sammy Cezanne drew on the driveway."

The police went over and looked at the chalk drawing on Sammy's driveway. "Did you do this?" one of the police officers asked Sammy.

He didn't know how to respond and muttered, "I, uhh, umm . . ."

The officer interrupted Sammy. "Where do you live?"

The boy pointed to his house next to the drive. The police noted that the writing on the sidewalk was chalk and not paint. They did not arrest Sammy, but they promptly took Rebecca Rembrandt down to the station and called her parents.

# What's Your Opinion?

1. How would you define *vandalism*?

**The Law Says:** Vandalism is the intentional destruction, damaging or defacing of someone else's property. Legally, vandalism is called "malicious destruction of property" or "malicious mischief." The crime may be either a misdemeanor or a felony depending upon the amount of damage.

2. Why did the police decide that painting on the school wall was a crime but writing on the driveway was not?

**The Law Says:** The chalk used on the sidewalk was not permanent and it would wash away in the rain. Paint, however, must be cleaned off the wall. Spray paint would have to be removed by the school custodian and would take hours of work and the use of solvents and cleaning compounds. Since the school district would have to pay the custodian to remove the graffiti, Rebecca's prank was costly. Sammy Cezanne drew the chalk pattern on his own property. A home owner has the right to alter his or her property in this way.

3. Is the breaking of windows in an abandoned house malicious destruction of property, even though no one lives there? Why?

**The Law Says:** Yes. That the house is abandoned makes no difference. The house is still someone else's property. The owner may plan to sell it, to rehabilitate it or move back in.

# What If?

1. **What If** Rebecca Rembrandt had written on the school wall in chalk instead of paint? Would that have made a difference?

**Answer:** This is not such a clear case of vandalism since chalk can eventually wear off the school wall. But the school principal might decide to have the custodian wash the chalk off the surfaces because it defaced the school. In that case, the time and money spent cleaning would be considered "damages" in a legal sense and could be prosecuted.

2. **What If** either Rebecca Rembrandt or Sammy Cezanne had drawn in chalk on a neighbor's sidewalk? Is that a crime?

**Answer:** The practical answer is that one must always ask permission of a property owner before doing anything that might be objectionable. Never assume that it is all right to post signs or draw pictures on any property that is not your own. If the neighbor objects to the "art," the artist could be prosecuted.

# Activities

1. Discuss: What are the costs of vandalism to society?

2. What is the difference between harmless pranks and vandalism on Halloween?

3. Write an editorial which protests malicious destruction of property and calls for a legal solution.

4. Look up the word *vandal* in the dictionary. What are its historic origins? (Also look up *Hun* and *Attila*.)

5. List all of the consequences of breaking a one dollar window in an empty house in the middle of winter.

**Answer:** The cold air could freeze the pipes and cause them to burst and flood the house. The water could short out the electrical system and cause a fire. Animals could get in through the broken window and cause havoc. Breaking a one-dollar window could cause the destruction of an entire house.

# Freedom of Speech/Freedom of Expression
## Case of the Green Arm Bands

A group of students in the Civics Club at Patrick Henry Middle School were concerned about the United States' nuclear arms arsenal. To show their support for peace and nuclear disarmament, they decided to attend school for one week wearing green arm bands.

Hearing of the plan and fearing that school would be disrupted, the principal, Ms. Gladys Grimm, made a rule against wearing arm bands.

In spite of the rule, some students came to school wearing arm bands anyway. The students were suspended. They sued the school district in federal court for violating their First Amendment rights.

**The students sued the school district for violating their First Amendment rights.**

# What's Your Opinion?

1. Read the Preamble to the U.S. Constitution and then read the First Amendment. (Both are in the Appendix.) List the freedoms guaranteed by the First Amendment. Why do you think that the authors of the Constitution considered those freedoms to be so important and fundamental? Why was it necessary to guarantee them in the highest law of the land?

**The Law Says:** The framers of the Constitution believed that these freedoms were absolutely necessary to "secure the blessings of liberty." To be truly free, the freedoms listed in the Bill of Rights (the first 10 amendments) are the most essential. The 13 colonies had just freed themselves from the tyranny of King George of England. The authors of the Constitution knew firsthand that the people must retain those rights, by law, to guarantee that the government could never deny those rights to the people.

2. Who will win the case—the students or the principal? Why?

**The Law Says:** The students will win. This case is based on an actual case that was eventually decided by the U.S. Supreme Court in Tinker vs. Des Moines School District 393 U.S. 503 (1969). The plaintiffs were John Tinker, 15; Mary Beth Tinker, 13; and Christopher Eckhardt, 15. They all opposed the participation of the United States in the Vietnam War. They were sent home from school after wearing black arm bands to express their opposition to that war. A lower federal court decided in favor of the principal. The students appealed and the U.S. Supreme Court, the highest court in the United States, reversed the decision of the lower court and ruled in favor of the students. The Supreme Court said that wearing arm bands was protected under the First Amendment to the Constitution, which guarantees freedom of speech. The court called the wearing of arm bands "symbolic speech." The court ruled that school officials could not prohibit such speech if the prohibition was merely to avoid peaceful discussion of legitimate topics of debate. Nor could the principal prohibit such a demonstration because of the vague fear that it might disrupt school. A mere possibility of disruption is not enough to deprive people of their rights to free speech. The principal could restrict a display only if one or more of the following conditions were true: (a) The display would certainly disrupt the operation of the school. (b) The protest would infringe on other people's rights. For the full text of the Tinker case, go to the Findlaw.com web site or directly to: http://laws.findlaw.com/us/393/503.html

3. Would it be proper for the principal to allow the wearing of political paraphernalia, buttons, bumper stickers, etc., only in the cafeteria during lunch hours but not allow it anywhere else in the school at anytime?

**The Law Says:** Perhaps. Reasonable rules can restrict the time, manner and place of free speech as long as the regulations do not apply to the subject matter and the reason for the rules is "compelling." For example, it would be legitimate for a city to make an ordinance prohibiting use of loudspeakers from 9 p.m. to 9 a.m. on city streets. It would not be legitimate to allow loudspeakers only to advertise one political party but prohibit it for another.

4. Do you think the Tinker case applies to all public schools? Why or why not?

**The Law Says:** Yes. Since the Tinker case was decided by the U.S. Supreme Court, the decision applies to all public schools in the United States. Private schools are not included in the Tinker decision because attendance at private schools is voluntary while attendance at public schools is mandatory.

5. Reread the First Amendment. This amendment guarantees freedom of religion to everyone, but it also prohibits the government from establishing any state-sponsored religion. Given that there is freedom of religion, if a student chooses to make a brief, private prayer in school, before class starts, can he or she do so?

**The Law Says:** Yes. The government cannot interfere with the free exercise of religion unless there is an overwhelming reason, known as a compelling state interest. On the other hand, the school or teacher cannot require, request or even suggest that students make any prayer, even if the prayer is completely optional. The courts have ruled that even optional prayers put impermissible pressure on students to conform and therefore violate the establishment clause of the Constitution. (The "establishment clause" is the clause that forbids the government from establishing an official religion.)

# What If?

1. **What If** the people wearing the arm bands blocked the doors to the school and other students were not able to enter? Would that be permissible?

**Answer:** No. The second part of the Supreme Court test was that protesters may not interfere with the freedom of other people who are not participating. Blocking the entrance would be improper.

2. **What If** the principal allowed students to wear arm bands but prohibited them from wearing buttons with political slogans, peace signs and witty sayings? Would this be valid prohibition?

**Answer:** No. Though only arm bands were the explicit subject in the Tinker case, all other forms of nondisruptive, nonobscene expression were clearly included in the decision.

3. **What If** instead of protesting nuclear war, the students wanted to wear swastikas to show their support for Hitler and his Nazi party? Could that be prohibited by the principal?

**Answer:** Perhaps. Even very unpopular opinions have the right to be expressed. This is difficult for many people to accept. Freedom of speech must extend to all opinions, both popular and unpopular, if we are to be truly free. However, wearing swastikas or Ku Klux Klan robes might be considered so provocative and upsetting that it would disrupt the school and could legally be prohibited by the principal.

# Activities

1. Post the First Amendment for the class. Brainstorm the following: Imagine what might happen if the First Amendment did not exist. Think about the abuses of governmental power that could result.

2. Hold a town meeting. Include people who support the position that school is not the place for political expression. Also include those who feel that students are citizens who have the right to express themselves on important issues, in appropriate ways, in school. Keep in mind that a principal must balance the rights of students and teachers to express themselves freely, with the need to maintain an effective educational environment. There is a sensitive balance between one person's right to free speech and another person's right to an orderly classroom where learning can take place.

3. In the Tinker case, Justice Fortas, writing for the majority of the Supreme Court, wrote: "Students do not leave their constitutional rights at the schoolhouse door . . . . Unless it is proven that the expression of opinion will create a substantial interference with schoolwork or discipline, students are entitled to freedom of expression of their views."

Is it possible that people will have different views of exactly what this means? With a partner, give some examples of what you think is an acceptable or unacceptable expression of opinion in a school setting. Is *substantial interference with school* easy or difficult to define?

# Activities

4. You Be the Judge: You are a municipal judge in the city of Anytown. Mr. Jerry Joker is brought before you by the Anytown Prosecuting Attorney. Mr. Joker is charged with a misdemeanor called reckless endangerment, because he allegedly yelled out "Fire" in a crowded movie theater as a prank. Several people were hurt in the panic that followed as they rushed to escape even though there was actually no fire.

At the trial, Mr. Joker admits he yelled "Fire" as a prank. But Mr. Joker and his attorney claim the law of reckless endangerment is unconstitutional because it deprives Mr. Joker of his First Amendment right to freedom of speech. Joker and his attorney also say the law is vague and too broad.

The prosecuting attorney notes that even free speech has its limits—especially where it endangers public safety.

As judge, you know that the U.S. Supreme Court has ruled that freedom of speech is called a "fundamental right." But the Supreme Court has also said that even fundamental rights may be limited where there is a compelling state interest (a matter of overriding importance which requires government intervention).

The Reckless Endangerment statute (law) reads as follows: "Anyone who shall incite a group of people to panic or riot by use of inflammatory or false statements shall be guilty of a misdemeanor punishable by not more than six months in jail and/or a $500 fine."

You be the judge. Write a legal opinion ruling on the constitutionality of the law. Is there a "compelling state interest" here? Also respond to Mr. Joker's argument that the law is vague and too broad.

5. **Bonus Question:** The First Amendment to the Constitution says: "Congress shall make no law . . . abridging the freedom of speech." The amendment refers only to the U.S. Congress. It does not say states cannot make such laws. The school district in the Tinker case was a state school in Iowa. Why did the Supreme Court decide that the First Amendment applied to states, too?

**Answer:** The Fourteenth Amendment reads, in part, "No State shall make or enforce any law which shall abridge the privileges or immunities of citizens of the United States . . . ." This makes all of the guarantees of the Constitution apply to state as well as federal government.

# Private Property/Trespassing
## Case of the Shortcut Caper

As usual, Willie Walker was in a hurry to get to the Anytown Shopping Mall after school. He knew he could save at least 10 minutes by cutting through the Baskerville's backyard.

Willie didn't know that the Baskerville family had just bought a really nasty watchdog. The Baskerville house had been burglarized, and they wanted a dog to protect their property!

Carefree, Willie leaped the fence into the waiting jaws of Fang, the hound of the Baskervilles. Willie barely escaped becoming Fang's afternoon snack!

He threw himself back over the fence with the dog's jaws firmly attached to his sneaker. His heart pounded against his chest as he finally escaped Fang's fearsome choppers. His jeans were shredded, he had lost one sneaker and he was scared out of his mind.

**Willie thought he'd save 10 minutes.**

# What's Your Opinion?

1. How would you define *trespassing*?
**The Law Says:** Trespassing is entry onto or interference with the property of another person without permission. It can be both a civil and a criminal violation.

2. Can Willie Walker sue the Baskervilles?
**The Law Says:** This is a trick question. Yes, Willie can sue. But will he win? Not likely. He is a trespasser and has very few legal rights in this situation.

3. Does it make a difference that the Baskervilles had a fence around their property?
**The Law Says:** Yes. The fence makes it clear that the owners do not want people going onto their property.

4. Shouldn't the Baskervilles have posted a sign saying, "No Trespassing" or "Beware of Dog"?
**The Law Says:** Not necessarily. Of course it never hurts to warn people of dangerous conditions, but a fence is as obvious as a sign. It means: keep out. If the family did not have a fence around their lot and it wasn't clearly private property, then a sign would be important to inform others of the dangerous dog.

# What If?

1. **What If** Fang attacked the newspaper carrier who was delivering the paper to the front door? Would the Baskervilles be liable then?

**Answer:** Yes. Especially if Fang had a history of biting people or being vicious. The law used to be that a dog would get "one free bite," before the owner became liable for its bites. The theory was that until the owner had reason to know the dog bit people, he wasn't negligent. Today most states hold dog owners to a higher level of responsibility for their pets' behavior. Also, in this case, the newspaper carrier was "invited" by the Baskervilles to deliver the paper. When you invite someone onto your property, you have a higher level of responsibility for their safety than to a trespasser.

2. **What If** a guest slips and falls on the Baskervilles' icy steps? Who would be responsible for the injuries?

**Answer:** The Baskervilles would be liable. Property owners have a legal duty to maintain their premises in a reasonably safe condition for the benefit of legitimate guests. Cleaning ice and snow from porches and walks is part of that duty in most states.

3. **What If** the Baskervilles tear down their fence and build a swimming pool in the backyard? One day some neighboring children sneak into the pool and one drowns. Would the Baskervilles be liable for the death of the child?

**Answer:** Yes, very likely, especially since they had removed the fence around their property. Things like swimming pools, large piles of dirt and discarded refrigerators are known as "attractive nuisances." The law recognizes that owners have special responsibilities to stop neighborhood children from being attracted to such dangerous areas.

# Activities

1. There is a tree in a neighbor's yard on the way home from school which is laden with big, luscious apples. The owner never seems to pick them and many are left to fall and rot on the ground. Nobody really seems to care one way or the other. Since the fruit is going to waste anyway, do you think you could help yourself to an apple by putting your arm through the fence? You wouldn't even have to go into the yard to get the fruit. Is this trespassing? Or is it something else? Write a paragraph that expresses your view of this.

   **Answer:** Reaching through the fence, if your arm crosses over the property line, is a trespass. Taking the apples, like picking a flower, is also larceny (theft). If the property owner complains to the police, you could be in trouble.

2. **Role Play:** If you were a defense attorney, how would you defend your apple-picking client on the basis that the property owner didn't seem to want the fruit? Prepare a convincing case for the court. If you were the prosecutor, what arguments would you make?

3. You Be the Judge: One dark midnight, Gertie Goofer breaks into a vacant house owned by Harry Hostile. Because the house has been repeatedly ransacked, Mr. Hostile has set up a booby trap. When Gertie enters the front door, she trips a wire connected to the trigger of a shotgun. The gun goes off, severely wounding Gertie. After getting out of the hospital, Gertie is tried and convicted of breaking and entering. This does not stop her from suing Mr. Hostile for the injuries caused by his booby trap.

   The case comes before you. You must find for or against Gertie in the civil lawsuit against Harry. Write the decision in the case of Gertie Goofer vs. Harry Hostile. Justify your decision.

   **Answer:** Mr. Hostile would be found liable for Gertie's injuries and would have to pay her hospital bills, at least. The logic: shooting someone for breaking into a vacant house is considered excessive force since it exceeds the punishment that the law allows. It might be a different matter if Mr. Hostile was in the house and thought his life was being threatened by a burglar. Refer to the assault and battery case.

4. Can you think of situations when necessity would be a defense for trespassing? Describe such emergencies in a brainstorming session.

5. How would you feel if it were permissible for anyone to walk on your property at anytime? List the reasons why you think "no trespassing" laws are important.

   **Answer:** To ensure personal privacy, to avoid the possibility that someone may be injured on your property for which you may have to pay, to guarantee the benefits of private property.

# Truancy
## Case of the Truant School Ghouls

A bunch of students at Anytown Middle School formed a club called the Ghouls. One beautiful spring day the Ghouls decided they would much rather play video games than be in school. In between classes they all slipped out a rear door when no one was watching and headed uptown.

While they were hanging out in Duke's Video Arcade, Officer Eagle-Eyes spotted them. He knew it was a school day and went up to ask them why they weren't in class.

Big Wilbur Windbag, the leader of the Ghouls, stepped forward. "Our teacher was sick and they couldn't get a substitute or anything, so class was dismissed early." He was very sincere.

Officer Eagle-Eyes was not convinced. He decided to take all five Ghouls into "custody" even though he wasn't sure that Wilbur's story was a lie. He took them back to school and into the office where the principal, Ms. Ruth Ruler, was extremely happy to see all of the Ghouls.

**Officer Eagle-Eyes was not convinced.**

# What's Your Opinion?

1. What is an arrest?
**The Law Says:** An arrest is the lawful deprivation of freedom to leave. One is under arrest if one is detained involuntarily or taken into custody.

2. How do you know if you are under arrest?
**The Law Says:** A police officer should tell you. If you are not sure, ask, "Am I under arrest?"

3. Can a police officer take a minor into custody even if the officer is not sure that the minor has committed a crime? Under what circumstances?
**The Law Says:** Yes. Although it is not a formal arrest, most states allow police officers to take juveniles into protective custody if they have reason to believe that the minor is in need of supervision (has run away from home, is skipping school or is in a dangerous situation). This is not a formal arrest, but it is effectively the same thing.

4. If a minor is arrested or taken into custody, what must the police officer do as soon as possible?
**The Law Says:** The police must call the minor's parents as soon as possible. In this case, returning the students to the custody of the principal is probably an acceptable alternative since school officials are considered to be in "loco parentis" (the legal equivalent to parents during school hours).

5. Could a police officer arrest or take an adult into custody if no crime was committed? Explain.
**The Law Says:** No. A police officer cannot arrest or search an adult unless the officer has an arrest warrant or search warrant signed by a judge or if the officer has "probable cause" to believe that a felony was committed and that the person about to be arrested committed it. (See also "Case of the Forgotten Fudge" and reread the Fourth Amendment to the Constitution.)

6. How would you define *juvenile delinquent*?
**The Law Says:** A juvenile delinquent is a minor who has committed a crime or violated the law. Juveniles who have not committed crimes but are having serious behavior problems, such as truancy or running away from home, are known as "minors in need of supervision" or M.I.N.S.

7. Who decides if a young person is a juvenile delinquent or a minor in need of supervision?
**The Law Says:** A special juvenile court judge would hold a hearing or trial to decide. Such a decision requires due process to safeguard the rights of minors.

8. What punishment could the Ghouls receive for cutting class?
**The Law Says:** If this was their first offense, the principal would decide on a fair punishment, such as extra work, suspension or detention hours before or after school. If the Ghouls repeatedly cut class, they could be tried in juvenile court and possibly be sent away to special schools for delinquent minors until they reach legal adulthood. In a growing number of states, the parents could also be held responsible for their children's failure to attend school.

# What If?

1. **What If** school had really been dismissed early and Wilbur Windbag had been telling the truth? Would Officer Eagle-Eyes be in trouble for his actions?

**Answer:** Probably not. The standard for taking juveniles into custody is so broad that it gives police a large amount of discretion for such behavior. As long as the officer acted reasonably under the circumstances, the officer would probably be immune from legal action.

2. **What If** the officer searched one of the Ghouls and found a bag of marijuana? Would he be able to charge the student with possession of drugs?

**Answer:** Such a charge would probably not hold up unless the officer had "probable cause" (a reasonable likelihood to believe that the student had committed a crime), before searching the student. A minor can legally be taken into protective custody under circumstances that would not merit a formal legal arrest. But a formal arrest based on probable cause is still required before searching a minor.

3. **What If** the officer had found a gun after frisking the students even though he hadn't formally arrested them but just took them into custody? Was the frisk legal?

**Answer:** Yes. The law distinguishes a "stop and frisk" from an "arrest and search." A police officer may frisk someone who is being questioned if the frisk is for the limited purpose of checking for weapons. This is justified on the grounds that the frisk is only to guarantee the officer's safety and the safety of others. However, if a weapon is found during the frisk, the person who possessed it may be prosecuted if the weapon is possessed illegally.

# Activities

1. Brainstorm answers to the question: Why did lawmakers of every state pass laws requiring children to attend school until they reach a certain age? The age at which students can drop out of school varies among the states. On the average, states require children to attend school until they are at least 16. In some states other factors are taken into account such as employment, completion of a certain grade, family economics and health reasons. What are the laws in your state regarding age and compulsory education?

2. **Role Play:** You are a counselor talking to a student who has been offered a job in a gas station. The student tells you that the owner has promised almost double the minimum wage and a steady 7 to 5 job starting next week. What good reasons could you give this person to encourage him or her to stay in school?

3. Organize research teams to find the statistics which indicate the expected annual income or lifetime income for high school dropouts, high school graduates, college graduates and trained tradespeople. What conclusions can be drawn from this information? Chart these facts for display.

4. **Role Play:** "Congress is now in session." Pretend that the members of the class are congresspeople. Divide into several "subcommittees." Have each subcommittee write a law which defines the powers of the police to detain juveniles under certain circumstances. Indicate the acceptable reasons for such detention, how long it can last, when parents must be called and under what circumstances the juvenile is to be released into the custody of his or her parents. Indicate at what stage of the process the courts are to be involved.

After writing the laws, have the committees introduce their proposed legislation to the "floor" of the Congress. Debate the different versions. Decide on one compromise bill. Have different congresspeople argue on behalf of parents, teachers, police officers, party store owners, students, principals, video arcade owners and other interested parties. After the debate, vote on the final bill.

TLC10242 Copyright © Teaching & Learning Company, Carthage, IL 62321-0010

# Equality Under Law/Civil Rights
# Case of the Super Students

On the first day of school after summer vacation, the parents and students at Bellwether High were invited to a special evening meeting. The results of that meeting shocked and surprised them. The Principal, Mr. Knowidall, announced that he had designed an innovative plan for all the Armenian students. Because of their academic superiority, they were going to be placed in their own separate classrooms.

Knowidall said that Armenians were generally better students because of their ethnic background and cultural values. Though his decision was not based on actual grades or test scores, he was sure his plan would enjoy the approval of the community.

As it turned out, the Armenian parents and students were extremely upset. At the next school board meeting they protested that they were victims of discrimination.

Mr. Knowidall defended his plan. "I'm doing this for your own good! This plan will let Armenian students accelerate their studies and at the same time protect regular students from feeling inferior," he said.

The spokesperson for the Armenian families disagreed. "Discrimination based on race or national origin will set these students apart socially and academically from their other classmates," she said. "We believe that segregating students based on race, ethnic background or sex violates the U.S. Constitution and is prohibited by the Civil Rights Acts passed by Congress of the United States."

Mr. Knowidall argued that although the students would be taught separately, they would all receive equal education.

**"I'm doing this for your own good!"**

# What's Your Opinion?

1. Is the principal's plan for separate but equal classes legal or illegal? Explain.

**The Law Says:** The plan is illegal. The United States Supreme Court answered this question in the landmark 1954 case of Brown vs. Board of Education of Topeka. 347 U.S. 483 (1954). You can read the case on the worldwide web at http://laws.findlaw.com/us/347/483.html. In that case, the court ruled that segregating students by race violates their rights to equal protection under the law guaranteed by the Fourteenth Amendment to the Constitution. In the Brown case, African American students in Topeka, Kansas, were denied admission to schools attended by white children until the courts intervened.

2. Since the Brown case was decided, the Congress of the United States has passed a series of civil rights laws that prohibit discrimination based on race, sex, religion or ethnic background. These laws prohibit segregation in all public institutions and all businesses that serve the general public. This means that schools, restaurants, hotels, buses, theaters, airplanes and all other facilities open to the public cannot make people of different races or sexes sit in separate locations or use different facilities. Why do you believe Congress passed this law?

**The Law Says:** All people must be treated equally under the law according to the Constitution. Segregating people robs them of the right to share all public facilities equally. Congress recognized that when separate facilities were provided for minorities, these facilities were never truly of equal quality.

3. Can you think of some facilities where it is legal to discriminate on the basis of sex?

**The Law Says:** Certain situations are obvious. For example, separate bathrooms for men and women are still allowed. Locker room attendants may be required to be the same sex as those who use the facility. Men and women may have separate sports teams as long as they are provided with equal programs and equal use of facilities. Since the Constitution guarantees freedom of religion, religious groups are free to make independent religious decisions. For example, some churches still prohibit women from becoming ordained members of the clergy.

4. What other kinds of rights do you think are protected by the Constitution and the civil rights laws?

**The Law Says:** All of the following are protected by civil rights laws and the Constitution:
1. The right to vote
2. The right to equal access to public facilities
3. The right to travel
4. The right to a free press
5. The right to associate with whom you please
6. The right to petition the government; to assemble peacefully
7. The right to own property
8. The right to buy a house in any neighborhood or city
9. The right to equal opportunities for employment
10. The right to worship

5. The civil rights laws have been extended to protect rights of the handicapped as well. How does the law assist the handicapped?

**The Law Says:** Facilities open to the general public are now required to remove barriers such as steps and narrow doors that block access to handicapped people. Also, employers are prohibited from discriminating against people with handicaps if they are able to do the job. Employers must also make reasonable accommodations for handicapped people.

78

# What If?

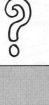

1. **What If** all the students in the Bellwether School System were tested for academic performance and, on the basis of the results, students were placed in regular or accelerated classes? Based on the tests, most of the students of Iranian origin were placed in the accelerated classes. Is the school district guilty of unlawful discrimination in this case?

**Answer:** No. In this case the students were separated on the basis of test scores only. Grouping people according to merit is legal as long as the tests are not biased in favor of one group over another. However, any testing or any program which seems to favor one group and/or exclude another would come under very close examination to be sure that the selection procedure gives everyone an equal chance.

2. **What If** a man and a woman score equally high on an employment test? The employer currently employs 50 men and two women. Is it legal, in this case to favor the woman applicant over the man if it is proven that in the past the employer refused to hire women based on their sex?

**Answer:** Yes. In cases where an employer's past employment practices have created a serious imbalance based on race or sex, then it is proper to take race or sex into account to remedy past unfairness. If both candidates are qualified for the job, the employer can choose the one to hire or promote based on sex or race, to correct past discrimination. This is known in the law as affirmative action.

# Activities

1. Only men are "drafted" (called to serve in the armed forces during times of war). The Supreme Court upheld the constitutionality of this policy. How do you feel about the fairness of having only men being forced to fight in times of war?

   Divide the class randomly into two groups, PRO and CON. Each group will stand at opposite ends of the room. All class members may participate by presenting arguments to support their respective group position, PRO or CON, re: Should women soldiers serve in combat? The point of this strategy is to be persuasive and convince members of the opposing side to join your ranks. Those who have changed sides may be given an opportunity to explain what convinced them to change their minds.

2. On occasion, even in this country laws are made which are later ruled to be unconstitutional. The process of overturning unfair laws is often a long and difficult one. Two examples of how unconstitutional laws can be changed lie in the history of the U.S. civil rights movement.

# Civil Rights Heroes

## Fred Korematsu

In 1944 Fred Korematsu was convicted of disobeying a Presidential Order. Fifty-four years later, in 1998, he was awarded the Presidential Medal of Freedom. Mr. Korematsu stood up for the civil rights of 112,000 Japanese American citizens and residents who were imprisoned without trials during World War II. President Bill Clinton presented the award, the United States' highest civilian honor, in an official White House ceremony on the birthday of the Reverend Martin Luther King, Jr.

On December 7, 1941, Japanese forces bombed the U.S. naval base at Pearl Harbor, Hawaii. The sneak attack killed and wounded thousands of U.S. servicemen. Much of the U.S. Navy Pacific fleet was sunk. Shortly thereafter, the U.S. Congress declared war on Japan, Germany and Italy.

In the throes of a war, President Roosevelt issued Executive Order 9066, known as the Exclusion Order. West Coast Japanese residents were relocated to camps in the desert for internment without trials or hearings. Seventy thousand of these were U.S. citizens. Many were children and elderly people. Many lost their homes and businesses. Other belongings were sold, given away or stolen. Fred Korematsu refused to go. Fred Korematsu was a U.S. citizen, born and raised in the United States. His family operated a nursery in Oakland, California. He was an American citizen. He wanted to help in the war effort but was treated like the enemy. He felt he was the victim of racism. He refused to go. He was arrested and convicted for violating the exclusion orders.

Sentenced to five years probation, he and his family were then sent to a camp in Utah. Tellingly, in upholding his conviction in 1944, the Supreme Court's decision never mentioned the words *equal protection,* although no German Americans or Italian Americans were similarly treated. Nor were there any reports of sabotage or terrorism committed by any Japanese Americans during that time.

Fred Korematsu never gave up his legal battle because he knew he was right. It was a long, difficult struggle. Finally, in 1984, the conviction was reversed.

A federal district court found the government's exclusion and detention actions during the war legally insupportable and violated the constitutional rights of Japanese Americans. Partially as a result, in 1988 Congress passed a bill in which the U.S. government apologized for the forced internment of Japanese American citizens and awarded each of them $20,000. Korematsu's case is now considered one of the most important legal cases in civil and minority rights.

At the White House award presentation ceremony, President Clinton said, "In 1942, an ordinary American took an extraordinary stand. Fred Korematsu boldly opposed the forced internment of Japanese Americans during World War II. After being convicted for failing to report for relocation, Mr. Korematsu took his case all the way to the Supreme Court. The high court ruled against him. But 39 years later, he had his conviction overturned in federal court, empowering tens of thousands of Japanese Americans and giving him what he said he wanted most of all–the chance to feel like an American once again. In the long history of our country's constant search for justice, some names of ordinary citizens stand for millions of souls: Plessy, Brown, Parks. To that distinguished list, today we add the name of Fred Korematsu."

## Rosa Parks

In the 1950s, a law in Montgomery, Alabama, required African Americans to ride in the rear of public buses. One day in 1954, a hard-working African American woman, Rosa Parks, after a long day of work, refused to give up her seat in the front of the bus to a white man. She felt that the law was wrong and decided to assert her rights. Her arrest led ultimately to that law being declared unconstitutional.

She was supported by the Reverend Martin Luther King, Jr., who led a boycott of the Montgomery bus system. Boycotts were also illegal under Alabama law. The civil rights workers at all times remained peaceful and nonviolent, even when violence was used against them. Ultimately, their courageous efforts were rewarded as old, unconstitutional laws were struck down and new laws passed to guard the civil rights of minorities and all Americans. Because these activists asserted their rights, those unjust laws might never have been changed.

# Activities

1. With regard to the case of the Japanese American internment during World War II and the laws which enforced segregation of African Americans in this country, discuss the following:

   Why is the price of freedom eternal vigilance?

   How are laws a reflection of the society that makes them?

   Why are laws only as just as the people who enforce them?

   Are those who sit idly by and allow injustice to occur as much to blame for society's injustices as those who actually commit them?

   When one person is robbed of his or her legal rights, how does this threaten everyone's rights?

   How can such injustice be avoided in the future?

2. Write a letter to your best friend. Pretend you are a U.S. citizen of Japanese descent living in San Francisco in 1943. Even though you were born in the United States, have never been to Japan and are a loyal U.S. citizen, you and your family are about to be sent to a detention camp. Your parents were forced to sell their business for less than it is worth. Your older brother is in the U.S. Army fighting for the United States at the same time the rest of your family is being deprived of their rights. Today is your last day of school in San Francisco before being sent away. What would you say in your letter to your non-Japanese friend so that he or she will understand how you feel? You are being taken away from your home and everything you have ever known for an indefinite time, as if you were a criminal. How would this disrupt your life? Why is it unfair?

# A Note

In 1943 Japanese Americans took their case to the U.S. Supreme Court. They argued that they were being singled out based solely on their race, which violated their constitutional right to equal protection of the law. Unfortunately, wartime hysteria prevailed. In 1944 the Supreme Court ruled against those U.S. citizens in the cases of Hirabayashi vs. United States 320 U.S. 81 (1944) (http://laws.findlaw.com/us/320/81.html) and Korematsu vs. United States.323 U.S. 214 (1944) (http://laws.findlaw.com/us/323/214.html).

Not all members of the court agreed. Three of the nine justices dissented. This means that they opposed the decision of the majority and wrote dissenting opinions. The dissenters wrote that the relocation law:

". . . goes over the very brink of constitutional power and falls into the abyss of racism . . . . To be valid, it is necessary only that the action have some reasonable relation to the removal of the dangers of invasion, sabotage or espionage. But the exclusion . . . of all persons with Japanese blood in their veins has no such reasonable relation . . . . There was no adequate proof . . . . Not one person of Japanese ancestry was accused or convicted of espionage or sabotage after Pearl Harbor while they were still free, a fact which is some evidence of the loyalty of the vast majority of these individuals. It seems incredible that it would have been impossible to hold loyalty hearings for the (individuals) involved–especially when a large part of their number represented children and elderly men and women. Any inconvenience (to the government) that may have accompanied an attempt to conform to procedural due process (by holding such hearings) cannot be said to justify violations of constitutional rights of individuals. I dissent, because I think the indisputable facts exhibit a clear violation of constitutional rights."

# Slander/Libel/Defamation of Character
## Case of the Math Menace

Maggie Metric was the very best math student in the class at Einstein High. Competitive excitement was running strong because of the announcement of a scholarship prize to be awarded to the math student with the highest cumulative grade for the year.

Lester Loutish was the strong second place student and was doing everything he could to beat Maggie for first place. The trouble was, he was not always the most ethical person in the world. Just before a big test, Lester got a brainstorm.

As Maggie, passed his desk, Lester whispered to her, "I hear you steal test answers from the teacher."

Flushed and angry, Maggie took her seat. She prepared for the test, deeply shaken by the awful lie! Encouraged with this bold strategy, Lester tried again on the day of the next big test. Before math class, he sneaked into the empty room and wrote in huge letters on the board, *Maggie Metric is a math cheat!*

In minutes, the entire class filed in and read the false message. When Maggie went in she broke into tears. The shocked teacher entered and briskly erased the board. Maggie was so rattled by the episode that she scored poorly on that day's exam. Because of her weak performance on that critical exam, she did not win the scholarship.

**Maggie Metric is a math cheat!**

# What's Your Opinion?

1. What civil law has Lester Loutish broken?
**The Law Says:** Lester has committed two torts against Maggie. (*Tort* is the French word for "wrong.") One tort he committed is called "intentional infliction of emotional distress." He is also guilty of "defamation of character," or libel. (Spoken defamation is slander. Written defamation is libel.) *Defamation* is defined as "a false statement about another person that is false or misleading and which damages the person's reputation when told to others."

2. Has Lester Loutish committed a crime against Maggie Metric?
**The Law Says:** No. Although he has violated civil law, his offense is not considered to be a criminal act.

# What If?

1. **What If** Lester Loutish made his false accusations directly to Maggie Metric's face, but no one else heard? Is this slander? Why?
**Answer:** No, it is not slander. To be slanderous or libelous, the false statements must injure one's reputation. To injure a reputation, the statements must be communicated to a third party.

2. **What If** Maggie proves that Lester's lies so upset her that she blew the exam and lost the scholarship and that his lies gave her a bad reputation? What remedies could a court award her?
**Answer:** A court could order Lester to pay Maggie an amount of money to compensate her for the damage to her reputation and an appropriate amount of money for the emotional harm done to Maggie. A court could also issue an *injunction* (court order which prohibits someone from doing something) ordering Lester to *cease and desist* (stop and discontinue) his harassment of Maggie. If Lester violated the cease and desist order, he could be fined or even jailed.

3. **What If** Lester Loutish heard a rumor that the mayor of Anytown had taken a bribe? Lester tells all his friends before he finds out that the rumor is false, and he stops circulating the lie. Can the mayor successfully sue Lester for defamation of character?
**Answer:** No. Public figures, such as politicians, receive less protection from libel and slander than people who are not in the public spotlight. To win a defamation suit, public figures must prove not only that the statements are false, but also that the person who made them acted with malice. *Malice* means that the person making the statements knew they were false and tried to intentionally injure the reputation of the public figure.

# Activities

1. Discussion: Why do you think it is a good idea to make it more difficult for public officials to successfully sue for defamation of character?

**Answer:** The U.S. Supreme Court answered this question in the case of New York Times vs. Sullivan 376 U.S. 255, (1964). The decision is available on the worldwide web at http://laws.findlaw.com/us/376/255.html. In setting the "actual malice" standard, the court noted two things: First, public officials themselves are granted immunity from libel lawsuits for false remarks they make (if made in the course of their official duties) unless made with "actual malice." Otherwise, the court reasoned, "the threat of lawsuits would inhibit the fearless, vigorous and effective administration of government." *New York Times vs. Sullivan, Supra.) Therefore, the court felt if public officials are immune from libel suits, so should those people be who criticize them in good faith.

The second point noted by the court was that if public officials could sue people for innocently made, though false, statements, then "would-be critics of official conduct may be deterred from voicing their criticism, even though it is believed to be true and even though it is, in fact, true, because of doubt whether it can be proved in court or fear of the expense of having to prove it in court."

If public officials could successfully sue people for making false statements made in good faith, the court felt it would "dampen the vigor and limit the variety of public debate. It would be inconsistent with the First and Fourteenth Amendments," New York Times vs. Sullivan, Supra.

2. **Two-Way Role Play:** Assign one student to play the President of the United States. Assign another student to play the editor of the *New York Times*. The President is furious because the *Times* just printed a story accusing him of illegal fund-raising. He wants the paper to print a retraction. The editor does not want to back down. He thinks the story is true, but it is hard to prove.

Play the scene twice. First, play it knowing the libel law as set forth in New York Times vs. Sullivan. Then play it as if the court had ruled that public official could sue newspapers and win defamation suits more easily. Hint: If the Sullivan decision had allowed defamation suits by public officials, the official would threaten the editor with lawsuits that would put his newspaper out of business. Thanks to Sullivan, however, the public official is limited to less coercive types of persuasion when dealing with the editor.

Note to the Teacher: You may choose to replace the President with a more current political figure in controversy or a different person in history or literature.

3. From your standpoint as a person knowledgeable in the law of defamation, what would you explain to someone who says, "Sticks and stones will break my bones, but names can never hurt me"? How can words hurt your reputation? What effects can this have on your life?

4. There is a frequently repeated quote that goes, "I don't care what you print about me as long as you spell my name right!" If you were to guess at the kind of person who would make such a remark, who do you think it might be? Explain the reasons for your answer.

5. Look up the word *reputation* in the dictionary. Why does the law protect a person's reputation?

Can you think of a situation where a famous person's reputation was damaged? How could such damage affect one's future?

# Property Rights
## Case of the Neighborly Nuisance

One warm summer night, Bad Boris Boombox decided to have a party. He called all his friends and by 11:00 that night everybody was rockin'. Everyone but Boris's neighbors, that is.

Boris's 10,000-watt stereo and his boisterous buddies frolicking on the front lawn were disturbing people for blocks. And the smoke from Boris's barbecue was wafting right into the open window of his neighbor, Fester Fusebox. Finally, Mr. Fusebox went ballistic.

He called Bad Boris on the phone. "Hey, Boombox, enough is enough." fumed Fusebox. "Your friends are acting like creeps; your stereo is keeping people awake for miles and the smoke from the barbecued goat is choking my whole family! Shut it down or I'll call the police!'

"Hey man, it's a free country," barked Boris. "I can do what I want on my own property. If you don't like it, close your windows."

The frustrated Fusebox finally called the police.

**The smoke wafted into Mr. Fusebox's open window.**

# What's Your Opinion?

1. Whose rights will prevail here? Boris's right to party or Mr. Fusebox's right to reasonable peace and quiet?

**The Law Says:** Mr. Fusebox has the right to peaceful enjoyment of his property—and more so late at night when we have expectations of quiet. Noise ordinances usually prohibit loud noise at night and early morning. Noise is measured in decibels. Decibel levels for different activities and times are regulated.

2. Boris's behavior is known legally as a "nuisance." Can you think of a definition of *nuisances* and list some?

**The Law Says:** A nuisance is any activity that disturbs or interferes with other people's rights to enjoy and use their own property. Loud parties, barking dogs, burning leaves and barbecues, smelly garbage piles, constantly noisy equipment, late-night disturbances, littering, and even letting weeds and grass grow too long, all can be nuisances.

3. What can Mr. Fusebox do to get Boris to be quiet?

**The Law Says:** If Mr. Fusebox calls the police, they will probably issue Boris a ticket or violation notice if the noise is still loud when the police arrive. Most cities have ordinances prohibiting loud noisemaking between certain hours and regulating activities that may become nuisances. Violating these ordinances may be civil infractions or misdemeanors.

# What If?

1. **What If** right after receiving the complaint from the neighbors, Boris turns off his stereo, moves his barbecue so it doesn't bother Mr. Fusebox and makes his guests quiet down? Would Boris still receive a ticket?

**Answer:** Probably not. If Boris promptly "abates" or eliminates the nuisance after being notified he is disturbing his neighbors, there is nothing more to complain about.

2. **What If** a nuisance continues for a long period of time even after a complaint? What can the neighbors do?

**Answer:** The neighbors could go to court and file a lawsuit against the offender. If the neighbors succeed, the court would issue a court order, known as an injunction, ordering a halt to the nuisance. Violating or ignoring the injunction could result in fines or even jail time for the offender.

# Zoning/Land Use Planning: Case of the Vanishing Farm

Farmer Fred owned a farm since 1959 where he grew crops and raised pigs and cows far from the city. He sold much of his harvest to people who lived in the city. By the year 2000, the city was at the doorstep of the farm.

Developers bought the farm next door. They tore down the farm, built houses in the meadow, put the babbling brook into a sewer and then named the subdivision Meadow Brook Farms.

After the homes were bought and families moved in, they complained that Farmer Fred was creating a nuisance. He often plowed his fields with a noisy tractor early in the morning. Even worse, his animals smelled and he sprayed chemicals on his crops which were carried by the wind to the new houses.

Farmer Fred was upset as well. "I was here first," he said. "Your fancy new houses have caused my taxes to go up and created dangerous traffic. Your kids are overcrowding my school. All your sidewalks and roads send runoff that floods my fields when it rains. And what will you city folks eat when you put all the farms out of business?"

Unfortunately, Fred was outnumbered by his new neighbors. They elected a township board that voted to make farming illegal.

Fred was forced to file a lawsuit. He claimed the government had effectively taken his land and not paid him. Fred's lawyer, Constance Tooshun argues that the board has violated Fred's right to due process in violation of the Fifth Amendment.

**". . . What will you city folks eat when you put all the farms out of business?"**

# What's Your Opinion?

1. Does the law making farming illegal violate the Fifth Amendment?

**The Law Says:** Yes. Read the Fifth Amendment. The anti-farming law effectively "takes" Farmer Fred's land without compensation.

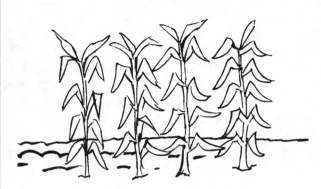

2. Does it make a difference that Farmer Fred was there first?

**The Law Says:** Yes. People who moved near the farm should have known that farms produce smells, noise and other things that could make it unpleasant to live nearby. The township board can make regulations to control nuisances and other activities. But as a matter of public policy, they cannot make necessary activities such as farming, electrical generation or manufacturing impossible, even if such activities create some problems. As a matter of equity, this is even more true when the subdivisions "go to the nuisance," rather than the other way around.

# Activities

1. Discuss the concept of "going to the nuisance" as illustrated by this story and why it might make a difference. Think about how we must balance the rights of property owners who have different interests from one another. Why does society have an interest in preserving farms even though it may not be easy to live next to them? How can laws help in such situations? Can you write a law that might help farmers survive?

2. Role-play a town meeting at which these issues are discussed. A chairperson calls the meeting to order with the following participants: Fred and other farmers, customers who eat Fred's crops, land developers, environmentalists and hunters who want to preserve open farmland and open spaces, construction workers, home owners and county officials. Try to mediate a solution to the problem.

3. Research the topic of "Disappearing Farmland." How serious is the problem? What is your state or other states doing about the problem?

88

# Role Play
# Congress Is Now in Session

*This role play could be divided into several sessions over several days.*

The goal of this exercise is to learn how laws are made. Students will write, debate and vote on a law. In this session, the goal is to write a law that will protect farms from encroaching suburbs.

The teacher is the "Speaker of the House."

Assign some students to be members of your state legislature. Assign other students to be "lobbyists" for different interests (see cue cards on pages 90-91). Have students wear name tags to identify their affiliations. The lobbyists try to convince the legislators to understand the position of their interest groups and shape the proposed legislation in their favor. You may duplicate the cue cards twice so every student has a role, or add/substitute other characters who would have local relevance.

1. Have every student in the class think of and write a law to protect farms and farmers from being put out of business or excessively regulated by encroaching suburbs.

Hints: Laws can take several approaches. You might want to have students research the problem in general. There are "right to farm" laws in several states today. Some laws reduce farmers' taxes even if land prices around them rise. Some laws allow farmers to sell the "development" rights (similar to mineral rights) to the state which makes them off-limits for housing. The law could reduce inheritance taxes if the farmer dies and wills the land to his children who wish to keep farming. (Otherwise the children often must sell the land to pay the inheritance taxes!) Some laws prohibit local governments from imposing any laws that are contrary to "standard" farming practices.

You can explain to students that farmers' taxes often rise when subdivisions approach because the value of the land rises and thus their taxes increase (especially since farms tend to have much more acreage than the average house lot). In addition, when new housing is built, someone has to pay for new roads and their maintenance; police, fire, EMS and social services for more people; bigger schools and libraries; water lines, sewer lines, garbage collection and waste water treatment for the expanded population. Paying for these items increases taxes.

The preamble to the law should read as follows:

BECAUSE farms are a necessary and important part of our state's economy, and

BECAUSE farmland is an important resource as the food source for the people of the state, and

BECAUSE farms are being endangered by growing suburban growth

THEREFORE, the People of the State of (   ) enact the following law:

2. Have each student read or post his or her proposed law for the other members of the class to study and think about.

3. Give the class 30 minutes to informally discuss the different proposed laws among themselves. The lobbyists try to talk with as many of the legislators as possible in the lobby to explain their positions. (Lobbyists got their name because they often talked to legislators in the lobby before votes were taken.) Students then share their views.

4. Have the class (Congress) reconvene. Hold a debate in which the legislators discuss and narrow the different laws down to one, using the best parts of all of the different proposals and adding amendments as necessary. (You may decide to limit debate to one or two minutes per legislator.) All the legislators may not agree. The teacher as "Speaker" will have final say over the wording of the final proposal. Write it on the board or prepare copies for the class for the next session.

5. The legislature has a final debate. Allow each legislator who wishes to speak one or two minutes on the proposed bill. Each legislator votes yes, no or "present but not voting" on the revised bill. After the final vote, you may have each participant read his or her cue card aloud to the class.

# Cue Cards

You are a legislator from an area that has many farmers. Your constituents who elected you want to see the strongest possible law protecting farmers and their rights to farm.

You are a legislator who accepts large donations from the American Farmers Association. You want farms to have control of their land so they can sell if they want but not be put out of business if they want to keep farming.

You are a legislator from an area that has many new housing developments. Housing generates taxes which you like. You think there are plenty of farms in the state and losing a few is no big deal. The people who elected you live in suburbs and are not concerned about losing a few farms.

You are a legislator whose family have been farmers for over 100 years. You argue that without farms we have no food. We must protect farms at all costs. Let people build new houses in areas other than prime farmland, such as in already existing cities. You favor a strong law protecting farmers' rights to farm.

You are a legislator who also owns a farm near a city. You have watched many of your fellow farmers sell their land for subdivisions. You think it is their own business if they want to sell their land so they can retire. But other farmers tell you they want to have a choice and not be forced out of business if they want to farm.

You are a legislator who thinks farms are important, and you don't want to see cities sprawling all over the land. You argue that urban sprawl has consequences that we all pay for such as the costs for fire and police protection, new schools, roads, sewers, water treatment plants and increased traffic.

You are a legislator who accepts campaign donations from a big housing developer. You want to keep him happy by making it easy for him to build big housing projects. You oppose legislation to protect farms. Argue that the free market should control whether farms stay in business or are forced to sell out.

You are a legislator who thinks farms are important to keep part of our land open and not overwhelmed with city sprawl. You argue that the state should buy the "development" rights from farmers so their land will remain farmland forever.

You are a legislator who lives in a suburb near a farm. You and your constituents do not like your children breathing in the dust that comes from plowing or the pesticides that float into your yard as the farmer sprays his crops. You want to limit the hours of operation of the farm so loud tractor noises do not wake you up at 5 a.m. You also want to control pesticide overspray.

You are a legislator who originally moved to this area many years ago so your children could go to a small but good public school away from urban problems.

You are a legislator who feels strongly that regulating land use infringes on (reduces) the right of individual landowners to use—and profit from—sale of or use of their property. You want no legislation.

You are a legislator who lives near a giant hog farm that bought out several smaller family farms years after you moved in. You want to regulate the size of mega-farm operations. You want to regulate the proper disposal of the manure so it doesn't run into the local streams and pollute the water and land and create horrible smells.

You are a legislator who has been trying to get businesses (which pay more taxes than farms) to move into the area but have not been very successful. One reason is that there is just not enough housing for more workers.

# Cue Cards

You are a lobbyist for a housing developer. You argue that the government should stay out of the free market economy. Argue that house building creates jobs for construction workers. A growing economy is a strong economy.

You are a lobbyist for an industrial food processor which owns a giant hog farm. You argue that giant hog farms make food cheaper because they are so efficient to operate. You want their right to operate protected.

You are a lobbyist from a state banking association. Your members want to increase their business by lending to new builders and new home buyers. You do not want to limit building new subdivisions.

You are a lobbyist from the League of Cities which does not want central cities to suffer as people move out to suburbs. You want to protect farms and keep population growth near the center of cities, not in suburbs. Therefore, you support laws that will protect farms from development

You are a lobbyist from the State Association of Realtors. You argue that house building is good for the economy because it employs carpenters and tradespeople. You say people should be able to build where they want. You oppose laws protecting farms.

You are a lobbyist from the Audubon Society. The law being debated will affect an area which is on an important flyway (bird migration path), and you are afraid that more development will affect both the wetlands where the birds stop to rest and the open fields at which they eat on their seasonal migrations.

You are a lobbyist from a state hunting association. You are very concerned that if more land is developed in the area, hunters will have no place to hunt. Already there have been many complaints from home owners who feel hunters come too close to their houses.

You are a lobbyist from a neighborhood group in one of the new subdivisions. You do not want more land developed because it will ruin your current views, and you are afraid that if low-cost housing developments are built it will drive down the value of your house.

You are an official with the Department of Natural Resources. You are concerned about the effect the big hog farms have on the water resources in the area. You are also worried about losing wetlands to development. The wetlands absorb rainfall and keep streams, rivers and floodplains from overflowing. Subdivisions with lots of paving add to flood problems because water runs off and is not absorbed.

# Privacy/Search and Seizure
## Case of the Unlucky Locker

One dismal Monday morning, a teacher, Mr. Sharpeyes, saw Kenny Compost put a toy gun in his locker. The teacher thought it might be a real gun and reported it to the principal.

The principal was quite alarmed. He had Kenny taken from class and demanded that he open his locker for an inspection.

When the search arrived at his locker, Kenny was so embarrassed by the incredibly dirty laundry and old lunches rotting in his locker that he refused to open the combination lock. The custodian was told to bring out the bolt cutters and, over Kenny's protests, began to cut through the lock.

**Incredibly dirty laundry was rotting in his locker.**

# What's Your Opinion?

1. Read the Fourth Amendment to the Constitution. Did the school have the right to search Kenny's locker without a warrant? Explain.

**The Law Says:** Yes. The principal had a very reasonable suspicion that Kenny had a gun. Another reason: the lockers actually belong to the school and not to the individual students who use them. The school has a responsibility to protect students. Some courts have stated that school officials are in "loco parentis" (in the place of the parent). Therefore, school officials have the right to search students' lockers just as parents do. More and more, however, school officials must use a standard of "reasonable suspicion" of illegal behavior before they can search an individual student—still a lower standard than the probable cause standard required of police for the general public. (See endnote.)

2. Privacy is known as a "fundamental right." The most important civil rights granted or implied by the Constitution are all known in the law as fundamental rights. List the rights you believe are fundamental and why.

**The Law Says:** The fundamental rights are freedom of speech, press, assembly and religion; the freedom to travel without restriction; the right to privacy; the right to marry and have children; the right to due process and equal protection under the law and the right to vote.

3. The Supreme Court has decided that the government can interfere with fundamental rights only where there is a compelling state interest. That means there must be an extremely important reason. What compelling reasons would justify regulations limiting freedom of speech? Freedom of religion? Freedom to marry?

**The Law Says:** Freedom of speech has been limited in cases where the speech incited people to violence or panic or involved a plan to overthrow the government by force or violence. Polygamy is illegal even though some religions permit it. Freedom to marry each other is not granted to brothers and sisters in order to avoid genetic inbreeding.

# What If?

1. **What If** the police arrived on the scene and proceeded to search all of the lockers without a warrant? Would they have the legal right to do that?

   **Answer:** No. The Fourth Amendment prohibits searches by police agencies unless they have a warrant signed by a judge or "probable cause" that a crime has been committed by the person they intend to search.

2. **What If** just as they enter the school, students are required to pass through metal detectors? Those students found with weapons are suspended or expelled from school after a hearing. Is this legal?

   **Answer:** So far, yes. This practice is used in several cities in the United States where guns in schools have created serious problems. Although some people criticize the practice as being an improper infringement of students' rights of privacy, the courts have not forbidden the practice. The U.S. Supreme Court has not ruled on the issue as of January 2000. (Research the status of such practices in your state.)

3. **What If** as a result of the locker search, the principal finds controlled substances (drugs, weapons) or other contraband in someone's locker? What could the principal do?

   **Answer:** The principal could (a) hold a hearing which could result in disciplinary action including expulsion, (b) call in the parents and/or (c) turn the material over to the police.

4. **What If** your father discovered something illegal in your dresser drawer and turned it over to the police? Is this legal? Can the police use the evidence against you in court?

   **Answer:** Yes. It is a legal search and the evidence is admissible in court. The "exclusionary rule" (See Glossary on pages 110-121) applies only to searches conducted by the police and the government, not to your parents.

# Activities

1. Discussion: Write a paragraph in answer to the following question: Why is it necessary for the police to have a warrant to search your home, yet no warrant or probable cause is necessary to search your luggage before boarding a plane?

   **Answer:** The privacy of one's own home is considered so sacred that the police may enter only with a search warrant, authorized by a judge. The airport, however, is a place where people do not expect the same amount of privacy. This is a case where individual rights must bend to the overidding need to guarantee the safety of all passengers. Also, airline personnel are not police and so are not required to obtain a search warrant to search those entering the airlines' private property.

2. Debate the following proposition: Terrorism is such a serious problem that the police should be allowed to search any home or any person at anytime, without a warrant, to combat the threat.

3. Discuss and/or write your views on these questions:
   a. Is it important to limit the power of the police? Why or why not?
   b. Can the police be limited in their power and still effectively fight crime and enforce the law?
   c. What would be the result of unlimited power by the police?
   d. What would result if there were no police force?
   e. How do we balance the individual's rights to privacy and the need of society to maintain order and enforce the law?

# Activities

4. Invite a police officer to your class to discuss the previously mentioned issues. Also contact the local branch of the American Civil Liberties Union and invite one of their members to discuss the same topics with your class.

5. Read and discuss the short story by Ray Bradbury, "The Pedestrian." Could this happen? Is it happening in some ways?

6. Where do we draw the line when we say, "the good of the group outweighs the rights of the individual." This position seems very sensible in the context of airport safety. But people concerned about "civil liberties" regard this as a dangerous first step toward a loss of other freedoms. Can you think of an example illustrating the dangers of the will of the majority destroying the rights of the individual? See Korematsu, Supra.

7. Many cities are installing television cameras, monitored by police in public areas. Do you believe this is a good or bad idea?

# For the Teacher

The Current State of the Law on Search and Seizure in Schools.

The question of whether Fourth Amendment protections against unreasonable searches and seizures applied to students when searched by school authorities was resolved in New Jersey vs. T.L.O. (1985). New Jersey vs. T.L.O., 468 U.S. 1214 (1984). (Available on the web at http://laws.findlaw.com/us/468/1214.html). In that case, a teacher found a student (called T.L.O. in the case, to protect her youthful identity) smoking cigarettes in the high school bathroom in violation of school rules. When taken to the assistant principal's office, she denied the accusation. The assistant principal opened T.L.O.'s purse, and found not only a pack of cigarettes but also marijuana, a large sum of money, a list of students who owed T.L.O. money and two letters that involved her dealing marijuana. When she was arrested on drug charges, she claimed that the evidence found in her purse should be suppressed as the fruits of an unreasonable search and seizure.

Since the Fourth Amendment only protects citizens against unreasonable searches and seizures by the government and its agents, there were two initial questions to be resolved. First, does the Fourth Amendment protect students from searches by school officials? It was decided that students subjected to school searches are, in fact, covered by the Fourth Amendment. For the first time, school officials were ruled to be closer to government agents than to parents.

The next question to be considered was whether the search was reasonable, as required by the Fourth Amendment. As discussed, the Fourth Amendment requires a warrant and probable cause before a search is considered reasonable. The court found that the Fourth Amendment's requirement of reasonableness was met if school authorities acted without a warrant, but with reasonable grounds for suspecting that the search would turn up evidence that the student has violated

or is violating either the law or the rules of the school. Such a search will be permissible when the measures adopted are reasonably related to the objectives of the search and are not excessively intrusive in light of the age and sex of the student and the nature of the infraction. In the T.L.O. case, all constitutional principles were found to be honored and the evidence of drug possession was admissible against the student.

In T.L.O. the "reasonable suspicion" standard was endorsed. It permitted school authorities to lawfully search students upon the passage of its two-pronged test: 1) The search must be reasonable in inception and 2) Reasonable in scope.

"Reasonableness" is the standard to justify a search. That is the key concept for school administrators. To ensure that the grounds used to suspect illegal behavior are reasonable, they should consider "the child's age, history and school record; the prevalence and seriousness of the problem in the school to which the search was directed; the exigency to make the search without delay and the probative value and reliability of the information used as a justification for the search" (State vs. McKinnon, 1977, cited in New Jersey vs. T.L.O. 1985, p. 737).

To ensure that the scope or implementation of the search is equally reasonable, school administrators must also limit the intrusiveness of the search in conformance with their reasonable assessment of the child's age, sex and the nature of the infraction.

# Due Process of Law/School Rules
# Case of the Suspended Student

Stanley Steadfast was walking to school one fine fall morning. His neighbor, Pedro Pyro, was burning a gigantic pile of fallen leaves. The smoke billowed from the fire and polluted the entire neighborhood. Stanley couldn't escape the smoke which clung to his clothing.

When Stanley walked into the school, he passed by the assistant principal, Mr. Stickler, who smelled the smoke immediately.

"Hey there, Steadfast," bellowed Mr. Stickler. "You've been smoking marijuana, haven't you?"

"No, sir. It was just leaves that . . ."

"Don't get smart with me, young man. Go to the office." The obedient Steadfast walked to the office, despite his innocence. Soon after, Mr. Stickler entered the office and announced, "Steadfast, you know that smoking marijuana is a crime. I'm expelling you."

"Don't I get a chance to explain?" pleaded Stanley.

"There's nothing to explain. I'm sorry, but rules are rules. I've got no choice."

**"Don't I get a chance to explain?"**

# What's Your Opinion?

1. Was Mr. Stickler's behavior appropriate?
**The Law Says:** No. Expulsion is a very serious punishment. Before a student can be expelled, he or she has the right to a fair and complete hearing. That is to say, the student has the right to expect due process of law.

2. What should such a process consist of?
**The Law Says:** The United States Supreme Court has ruled that if the suspension is for 10 days or less, the student must be informed, orally or in writing, the exact charges being made against him and the evidence the authorities have. The student must also have the opportunity to present his side of the story (Goss vs. Lopez, 419 U.S. 565 (1975) on the web at http://laws.findlaw.com/us/419/565.html).

For suspensions over 10 days, or for total expulsion from school, a more formal procedure may be required (Goss vs. Lopez, supra). Such process could include a hearing in front of an impartial fact finder, and perhaps allow the student to be represented by an attorney at the hearing. The exact process will vary from state to state.

The court has ruled that education is a legal right that cannot be taken away without due process of law. For further information, refer to the home page of the American Civil Liberties Union at http://www.aclu.org/

# What If?

1. **What If** Stanley Steadfast was expelled after a hearing but still wanted to prove his innocence? What could he do?

   **Answer:** Eventually Stanley might have to file a lawsuit in court. Before he can do that, however, he must first go through all of the normal channels and appeals with the school's administration. (This is known as "exhausting the administrative remedies.") He should appeal his case in writing to higher school officials, such as the principal and the school board. It would probably be worthwhile for Stanley and his parents to hire an attorney as early in the process as possible.

   If Stanley is unsuccessful with the school officials, then he might consider filing a lawsuit. Although this might be a costly and time-consuming process, the issues are serious enough and Stanley's case is strong enough that it might be worth the fight. He might get the American Civil Liberties Union to assist him.

2. **What If** Mr. Stickler actually saw Tommy Toker smoking marijuana in the parking lot and confiscated a bag of alleged marijuana from him? Could Tommy be expelled without a hearing in that case?

   **Answer:** No. Even in a clear case, the student is still entitled to a hearing (due process).

3. **What If** Penny Peashooter is firing paper wads at the back of Billy Bumpkin's head? Mr. Niceguy, the teacher, has been warning Penny all period to cut it out. Finally, in exasperation, Mr. Niceguy says, "OK, that's it! Go to the principal's office right now for your disruptive behavior." "I don't have to," says Penny, "I demand due process. A jury trial and an attorney." What are Penny's chances of avoiding an immediate trip to the office?

   **Answer:** Slim to none. Although Penny would be entitled to due process if threatened with suspension or expulsion, the teacher has the right to keep order in the class. Students have the responsibility to respect the rights of others. If the teacher attempts to remove the student for long periods of time, then the punishment begins to resemble a suspension which would require a hearing of some sort with other school officials.

4. **What If** school officials decide that, because of a serious drug problem in school, to reduce the use of illegal drugs they will begin random drug tests of student athletes' urine. Is this legal?

   **Answer:** Yes. The U.S. Supreme Court recently allowed the practice in the case of Veronia School. Dist. 47J vs. Acton (94-590), 515 U.S. 646 (1995) (http://laws.findlaw.com/US/000/U10263.html). The court ruled that 1) Urine drug tests are considered a search; 2) It is reasonable in this case because school athletes' expectation of privacy is already low because they take communal showers and must take physical exams before they are allowed to play; 3) Being forced to give a urine sample is a minimal invasion of privacy; 4) The state has an important interest in keeping students, especially student athletes, free of drugs.

5. **What If** school officials decide to use dogs to sniff out guns and drugs in student lockers?

   **Answer:** A fascinating web site regarding students' rights, Galt Union School District Drug dog lawsuit, (http://www.softcom.net/users/kareed/) shows how that case was resolved.

# Activities

1. Hold a debate. One side will take the position that to maintain discipline in the schools, the principal and the teachers should be free to expel and suspend students at will. The other side will argue that in school, as in society, a student is innocent until proven guilty and to shortcut due process is as unacceptable in school as it is everywhere else.

2. Stanley Steadfast's parents are convinced that their son is innocent. His dad believes that an innocent person does not need a lawyer to represent him. His mother believes that he does need a lawyer. Put yourself in the place of either parent and write a page explaining your position. Who do you think is right? Read your position papers in class.

   Argument for the dad's position that a lawyer is unnecessary: He would like to believe that the truth will come through and that it should not be necessary to call in an outsider. He might also argue that when you hire an attorney it appears as if you are guilty and that's why you need a lawyer. Also, some people believe that an attorney will unnecessarily inflame the situation.

   Argument for the mom's position that a lawyer is necessary: By hiring a lawyer, the other side will know that you are very serious about defending your rights. A lawyer also knows the important details of the law that can help make your case more forceful. It helps to have someone be your advocate and speak for you who is not so emotionally involved with the situation.

3. Ask the principal or assistant principal to come to your class to discuss disciplinary rules for your school. Prepare questions in advance regarding due process.

4. What if Stanley Steadfast asked you to defend him against the assistant principal, Mr. Stickler? What are some of the arguments you would use to convince a committee of your friend's innocence? Why is the case against Stanley a weak one?

# Substance Abuse
# Case of the Doubtful Dopers

After the high school dance, someone made arrangements for a party to wrap up the evening. Sid Smarm, one of the students, rented a room at the Sleazy Rest Motel and invited the most popular kids.

Word spread and dozens of students showed up—many uninvited! Some were drinking beer. Everybody was in good spirits when, out of the blue, someone started smoking marijuana and passing joints around.

Most of the kids weren't smoking and were looking pretty uncomfortable, but nonetheless, they didn't leave. Nobody wanted to walk out on a party of the elite and look like wimps.

The odor of the marijuana soon wafted through the motel hallways, and the owner was alerted by a concerned guest. The owner called the police who arrived promptly on the scene and arrested everyone in the room.

Several of the students protested vigorously that they were not smoking or drinking at all. The police continued to round up everybody in the room and said unsympathetically, "Tell it to the judge!"

**Sid rented a room at the Sleazy Rest Motel.**

# What's Your Opinion?

1. What crimes were committed by the students?

**The Law Says:** 1. Those who were actually smoking the marijuana were guilty of possession or use of a controlled substance; 2. Any students who were underage and were drinking alcoholic beverages were minors in possession of alcohol; 3. Anyone over the legal drinking age who supplied beer to underage students is guilty of contributing to the delinquency of a minor, which may be a felony; 4. Those who supplied the marijuana to others are guilty of a felony.

2. Were the students who were not smoking guilty of a crime?

**The Law Says:** Even those students who were not smoking pot, but who knew that marijuana was being used, could be guilty of "frequenting an establishment where illegal activity occurred" (a misdemeanor).

# What If?

1. **What If** the case of all the students came to trial and the nonsmokers were also accused of marijuana possession? Can the nonsmokers be convicted?

**Answer:** Yes. Even the nonsmokers can be convicted if the judge or jury does not believe that they were indeed just hanging around and watching the smokers!

2. **What If** you innocently find yourself in a place where there are drugs, alcohol, firearms or stolen merchandise? How can you protect yourself?

**Answer:** The practical answer here is that the only way to avoid such legal entanglements is to leave the premises immediately at the first sign of illegal behavior.

# Activities

1. How would you explain to someone in your class, who is really naive, all the things that could happen to a person from using illegal drugs?

**Answer:** A person could be fined, suspended from school, have a serious blemish on school records, be jailed or become addicted. Even if you are not caught, drugs can affect your grades, personality and emotional and physical health.

2. Role-play a situation where a student in your school is really trying hard to convince you to buy or try an illegal substance. How would you discourage him? What would be the best way to deal with the situation? What arguments would the pusher use?

# Copyright/Plagiarism
# Case of the Cartoon Copycat

Pedro Picasso was the best artist in the whole school. Everyone admired his great drawings. His favorite subjects were other students and teachers whom he would capture in various funny poses.

One day the governor of the state came to speak to an assembly in Pedro's high school. Pedro drew a pencil sketch of the governor as he spoke to the students. It was a very good likeness in Pedro's usual humorous style. He drew the governor's ears slightly larger than they actually were and his bushy hair wilder than real life. Everybody loved it.

To make sure he got credit for his drawing and to make sure no one would copy it without his permission, Pedro signed his drawing at the bottom with the following notice, "Copyright 2001 Pedro Picasso." Then he tacked a copy of the sketch on the school bulletin board.

The next day, Manny Moneymaker made a copy of Pedro's drawing on a copy machine and sold it to a local newspaper, which printed it in the newspaper, complete with Pedro's copyright notice at the bottom.

**Picasso was the best artist in the whole school.**

# What's Your Opinion?

1. Copyrights are the legal rights granted by Congress to artists, authors, music composers and creators of original works. Copyrights give the creators and their agents the exclusive right to use, sell or copy their work for their lifetime, plus 50 years. Why do you think Congress created copyrights?

**The Law Says:** If creative people could not control the fruits of their labor, their incentive to create would be reduced. Hence, Congress wrote the copyright law to protect what is known as "intellectual property." Intellectual property refers to inventions, compositions and original works of art or literature.

2. Did Manny Moneymaker violate the copyright law? Did anyone else?

**The Law Says:** Yes. Manny committed copyright infringement and so did the newspaper! This means that Manny illegally sold Pedro's property by reproducing and selling it without permission. The newspaper should have checked that Manny had Pedro's permission since there was a copyright notice right on the drawing! Pedro could claim money damages from both Manny and the newspaper.

3. Why was it necessary for Pedro to put his copyright notice on his drawing to preserve his copyright?

**The Law Says:** Notice is a very important part of the law. The copyright notice tells the world that Pedro intends to assert his rights. The notice must be placed where it can be clearly seen, otherwise the copyright is not good. If Pedro, or any artist or author, publishes his work without putting the notice on it, the work may become "public domain" (public property free for all to use). Anyone is free to use public domain works.

4. What remedies can Pedro seek from Manny and the newspaper for illegally using Pedro's cartoon?

**The Law Says:** If Pedro had filed his copyright with the Register of Copyrights in Washington, D.C., he could file a lawsuit against Manny and the newspaper. Pedro would be entitled to any money Manny received. Pedro could also obtain an injunction (a court order) prohibiting Manny from using Pedro's drawing. It is likely that both Manny and the newspaper would receive a fine, paid to Pedro for intentional infringement.

# What's Your Opinion?

5. What is *plagiarism?*
**The Law Says:** Plagiarism is a form of cheating. It is defined as "claiming someone else's work as your own." Copying from a book without giving the author credit is plagiarism. So is copying someone else's homework or test answers.

6. Is plagiarism a violation of the law?
**The Law Says:** Yes. Plagiarism is a form of fraud. Fraud in this case is defined as "unlawfully obtaining something of value by deception, lie or trick." When a student plagiarizes, he or she is trying to fraudulently obtain a grade or a diploma or a college degree. Plagiarism is also a violation of the copyright law if the plagiarized work has a copyright. Plagiarism is a violation of school rules because it violates educational ethics of honest scholarship.

7. What penalties may teachers or school officials impose from plagiarism?
**The Law Says:** Teachers and school administrators are free to judge each case. They are limited in three ways: 1. They must treat all students the same for similar infractions; 2. There should be a fair process to avoid punishing an innocent person; 3. The punishment should not be excessive.

Punishments can vary from lowering a grade on a single paper or test, failing a class or all the way to expulsion from school in extremely serious cases in colleges or universities.

8. What is the difference between a copyright, patent and trademark?
**The Law Says:** Copyrights give creators of original artistic, literary and musical works the exclusive control over their works for the lifetime of the author plus 50 years. Patents are granted to inventors of new and useful inventions. Patents give inventors exclusive control of their inventions for 20 years. Trademarks are the symbols, logos, labels and brand names that identify and distinguish one product from another. Trademarked goods are marked with the symbol TM or ® (meaning registered trademark). Trademarks are good as long as the product is sold in commerce.

Patents, trademarks and copyrights all fall under the category of "intellectual property" and are granted by the U.S. government in Washington, D.C.

# What If?

1. **What If** you are writing a research paper on American poets? In the course of your research you want to copy poems from different books, but you see that there is a copyright notice in each of the books and a statement which prohibits copying. Can you legally make copies or include those poems in your paper?

**Answer:** Yes. The copyright law makes a specific exception for scholarly and educational copying which is not done for profit and does not reduce the profits of the author. This is known as "Fair Use." Making multiple copies and distributing them to a whole class without explicit permission goes too far! And it is always required to give *full credit* to any author or poet whose work you copy.

2. **What If** you have written a rock and roll song that you want to send to your favorite group or to a music publisher? How can you protect yourself and avoid a rip-off?

**Answer:** This is one case where filing a formal copyright application with the Register of Copyrights in Washington, D.C., would make sense to protect your work. Also, it is extremely important to place the copyright notice on your work before showing it to anyone. The reason for filing a formal copyright application is to prove the exact date you published your work. Another way to prove the date of your publication is to have the original song notarized and dated by a Notary Public.

Warning: People often think they can prove the date of their creations by mailing a copy of their work to themselves. Most courts do not accept the mail technique as a valid date marker.

# Activities

1. Assert your legal rights! Produce a short story, a poem, a song, a cartoon, a blueprint, an original dessert recipe or a picture of your very own clown face. (Yes! Clown faces are copyrightable.)

   In order to be valid, a copyright notice must use the word *copyright* or use the letter *c* in a circle (©) followed by the year of the first publication and the name of the holder of the copyright. The holder who is the owner of the copyright may be the author or someone to whom the author has sold the rights, such as the publisher. Look inside a book on the title page to see how this information is recorded. If you want more protection, you must file your copyright with the government. You have several years after your first publication to actually file your copyright if you have applied the notice.

   For information, write to the Copyright Office, Library of Congress, Washington, D.C. 20540 or see the following web sites: U.S. Copyright office official web site: http://lcweb.loc.gov/copyright/ and The Copyright web site: http://www.benedict.com/ and the Patent and Trademark office official web site: http://www.uspto.gov/

2. **Role-play** scenes from the following situation: Valerie Volley is the school tennis champ. The athlete is doing poorly in one of her classes, though she's really working her head off. On Monday night, Valerie calls her friend Wally Goodheart because she is desperately in need of help. "I've got this paper due on 'Honesty,' and it's just about killing me," she tells Wally. "I keep writing it over and over, but it's still as clear as mud! You've got to help me."

3. A group of students are preparing speeches and dramatic interpretations for a school contest. The best presenter is using a speech from an old book she found and is pretending that it is her own original work. Only you recognize the speech as the work of another author. Despite the hard work of all the other students, this girl is going to win easily because the speech is so funny and professional. What is your responsibility in the matter? What would you do?

# Freedom of the Press
## Case of the Censored School Paper

Principal Robert Reynolds' eyes must have bugged out when he read a draft copy of the Hazelwood High School student newspaper, *The Spectrum*. One article started out like this:

"Sixteen-year-old Sue had it all–good looks, good grades, a loving family and a cute boyfriend. She also had a seven-pound baby boy." The article went on to discuss topics of teen sex and birth control.

His blood pressure certainly zoomed when he saw another article on the effects of divorce on Hazelwood students that used the names of the students and parents without their permission!

The principal made a decision: the articles were not to be published. He did not want to offend the named parents. He was also afraid that the discussion of sex was not appropriate for younger students.

The student editor of *The Spectrum*, Cathy Kuhlmeier, disagreed. She and her parents felt that their rights under the First Amendment of the U.S. Constitution had been violated because the school newspaper was a public forum.

The Kuhlmeiers and other students filed a lawsuit in U.S. District Court. The judge ruled against the students. The students appealed to the U.S. Court of Appeals in St. Louis which reversed the lower court. But the school district did not give up. THEY appealed to the United States Supreme Court which decided the case in 1988: Hazelwood School District vs. Cathy Kuhlmeier et al. 484 U.S. 260, (1988). Are student newspapers protected by the First Amendment?

**The principal made a decision: the articles were not to be published.**

# What's Your Opinion?

1. What's your opinion? Do you think a high school newspaper is different from other newspapers with regard to censorship?

**The Law Says:** Yes. The U.S. Supreme Court in Hazelwood vs. Kuhlmeier, previously cited made the following rulings: 1. Public school students' rights to free speech are not to be as extensive as adults'; 2. School officials may impose reasonable restrictions on the speech of students, teachers and other members of the school community; 3. School officials may control content of a school newspaper when the production is part of the regular educational curriculum.

# What If?

1. **What If** the students printed their newspaper independently in Cathy's basement? Could the school prohibit its publication or distribution?

**Answer:** No. If the students printed the paper on their own time, with their own money and not as a school-sponsored activity, the school has no say in the activity off school grounds. But the school may be able to control distribution of the paper on school property.

2. **What If** Cathy and her classmates print an independent newspaper in her basement which is critical of the Supreme Court's decision and the principal's censorship? The principal sees a copy of the paper at a local store and suspends the students. Is this legal?

**Answer:** No. The principal's behavior is not legal. Students' free speech rights outside the school are the same as all other citizens. Even if the article is untrue or defamatory, the principal has other remedies not including suspension or expulsion from school. The principal's remedies may include money, but the defamation must be intentional, since school principals in most states are considered public figures as to their work and therefore have a higher burden of proof in defamation cases. See the Case of the Math Menace.

# Activities

1. A concerned mother, Priscilla Prude, read an article about all of the bad things that can be found in Grimm's Fairy Tales. Mrs. Prude was horrified to read the list of violent incidents which appear in those stories. She decided to organize a school council meeting to encourage library reform by cleaning up and pulling out such material from the school library to protect the minds of little people.

Read some Mother Goose rhymes and some Grimm's Fairy Tales. Organize the class into groups representing parents, teachers and librarians in the community. At this meeting take a position for or against Mrs. Prude's plan to censor Grimm or Mother Goose. Have specific examples from Mother Goose or Grimm's Fairy Tales which could be viewed as having a bad influence on little children.

Another choice: Some parents want to ban the Harry Potter books by J.K. Rowling from schools because they feel the books promote witchcraft. Hold a debate on that issue using the same players as above.

# Activities

2. The third week of September is set aside by the American Library Association to observe Banned Books Week. It is a reminder that censorship goes against the precepts of the Constitution and that the efforts to ban and censor books and otherwise stifle free expression are as vigorous as ever. We are reminded that the *Holy Bible* is the most banned and burned book in history. Challenges and demands for censorship come from many sources, especially those who are concerned about young people.

Over the years, books of all kinds have been the target of people who want to censor reading material. These groups have different interests and different points of view. The motivation may be political, religious, educational or ethnic. Some may be concerned about ageist, racist and sexist literature.

To obtain a list of banned books or challenges which have occurred against books in the U.S., ask your school or public librarian, or write to: Director of the Office for Intellectual Freedom of the American Library Association, 50 East Huron St., Chicago, Illinois 60611. Their web site can be found at http://www.ala.org/. For the latest banned books, use the links "advocacy," "fight censorship" and "Banned Book Weeks press kit."

3. "Censorship: Good or Bad?" Organize groups in class for the purpose of discussing censorship. Should it be allowed or not? If we are to allow censorship, who will do the censoring for all of us and what material will be censored or forbidden? Is it difficult for people to agree? Isn't this part of the problem of censorship? Why do we say that if we allow any censorship we are on a "slippery slope"?

4. Some books censored have included: *Huckleberry Finn* by Mark Twain; Anne Frank's *Diary of a Young Girl*; *In the Night Kitchen* by Maurice Sendak (a picture book for children); *Making It with Mademoiselle* (a pattern book for dressmaking students published by *Mademoiselle* magazine); *The Autobiography of Ben Franklin*; *To Kill a Mockingbird* by Harper Lee; *Animal Farm* by George Orwell; *Great Expectations* by Charles Dickens; *King Lear* by Shakespeare; *The Red Badge of Courage* by Stephen Crane; *A Separate Peace* by John Knowles and *Little Black Sambo*. Interestingly, *Fahrenheit 451*, the classic book by Ray Bradbury, which has also been censored, is an allegory about book burning in a repressive society. The title refers to the temperature at which paper ignites and burns.

Ask your librarian how Banned Books Week is observed in your school library. The U.S. Supreme Court ruled on book banning in the case of Board of Education, Island Trees Union Free School District No. 26 vs. Pico, 457 U.S. 853 (1982). It is summarized in the Freedom Forum web site through the ALA web site (at http://www.ala.org, then use the links "Library Advocacy and Support," "Fight Censorship," "First Amendment," "First Amendment Advocates," then "Freedom Forum"). The case itself can be found at http://laws.findlaw.com/us/457/853.html.

5. Dozens of organizations are fighting to protect the First Amendment. To see this list of organizations, go to the American Library Association home page at http:/www.ala.org and use the links "Library Advocacy and Support," "Fight Censorship," "First Amendment" and "First Amendment Advocates." What do all of the agencies listed there have in common?

6. Here is a very hard question for discussion. There are books and web sites that describe how to make explosives and bombs. Should this material be available to children? Should it be available to anyone?

# Glossary of Legal Terms

## A

**abate** (verb). To end or eliminate. As: to abate a nuisance.

**abridge** (verb). To curtail or restrict. As: to abridge freedom.

**abuse** (noun). Improper, or unlawful use of authority. Abuse of discretion by a judge in a court action is an error which may require reversal or alteration of a ruling. Physical abuse of a child, spouse or domestic animal is a criminal offense. (verb). To hurt, injure or misuse.

**acceptance** (noun). In contract law, the formal response to an offer. When the acceptance reaches the offerer, a contract is created.

**accuse** (verb). To charge with a crime or other improper behavior.

**acquit** (verb). To find a person innocent of a crime after a trial. To find an accused person to be not guilty. As: he was acquitted by the jury.

**adjudicate** (verb). To decide a case after a legal proceeding. To judge.

**admissible evidence** (noun). Facts, testimony or objects legally usable to prove a case in court.

**admission** (noun). A statement by a party acknowledging guilt or responsibility in a civil or criminal case.

**adopt** (verb). To legally assume the role of a parent. To incorporate a fact, idea or philosophy as one's own.

**adversary** (noun). An opponent.

**advocate** (verb). To publicly support or argue for a cause or person; (noun) a person who publicly supports a cause. A lawyer is an advocate.

**affidavit** (noun). A signed statement which the maker swears is true in the presence of a notary public or court officer.

**affirm** (verb). To uphold or support. An appeals court will affirm a proper decision of a lower court or reverse an improper one. (See *appeal*.)

**affirmative action** (noun). The remedy used to correct past discrimination in hiring, firing and promoting or other opportunity in employment, education, housing, etc., which was based upon race, sex or national origin.

**age of majority** (noun). The age at which one becomes a legal adult. The legal voting age which is now 18.

**agent** (noun). A person or employee authorized to act in one's behalf.

**alias** (noun). An assumed name.

**alibi** (noun). A defense to a crime in which the defendant claims to have been somewhere else when the crime was committed.

**allege** (verb). To assert that a statement is true.

**allegation** (noun). An assertion or charge.

**amendment** (noun). An addition, correction or deletion in a legal document.

**answer** (noun). A formal response to a lawsuit or criminal complaint.

**appeal** (noun). The request made to a higher court to reverse the decision of a lower court. (See *grounds for appeal*.)

**appeals court** (noun). Also known as appellate court. A court designated to review the decisions made by lower courts at the request of a party. An appeals court will either affirm (uphold) or reverse (overrule) the decision of the lower court.

**appellant** (noun). The person bringing an appeal.

**appellee** (noun). The person defending against an appeal.

**arrears** (noun). A past due debt.

**arrest** (verb). To deprive a person of his or her liberty by legal authority. To physically take a person into custody.

**assault** (noun). The threat to strike another person which is reasonably believed by that person to be imminent. An attempted battery (striking or injuring of another person). The threatening action that precedes a battery.

**attempt** (noun). An act, beyond preparation, in pursuit of a crime. An attempted crime is a separate offense from the crime itself.

**attorney** (noun). A person given legal authority to act on another person's behalf. A lawyer.

# B

**bail** (noun). Money or other refundable security posted to insure that a defendant will appear in court at a later time. Judges usually set the amount of bail. (See the *Eighth Amendment of the U.S. Constitution*.) (See also *bond*.)

**bailiff** (noun). An officer of the court who keeps order in the court, "swears-in" witnesses and helps carry out a judge's orders.

**battery** (noun). A nonconsenual touching which harms another.

**bench** (noun). The place in the court where the judge sits. As: "Approach the bench, counselor." The collective name for members of the judicial branch of the government.

**bench warrant** (noun). An order issued by a judge for the arrest of a person.

**beyond a reasonable doubt** (adverb). The standard of proof necessary to convict a criminal defendant. A standard requiring very high certainty of the guilt of the defendant.

**bill** (noun). A legislative proposal submitted for approval. In business, a request for payment. In law, a written request or order.

**Bill of Rights** (noun). The first 10 amendments to the United States Constitution outlining the legal and civil rights of individuals.

**bond** (noun). Security posted for bail or for a debt. (See *bail*.)

**boycott** (noun). A group effort to stop all commercial transactions with a specified business, person or country.

**breach** (verb). To fail to perform as promised or required. To break. As "to breach a contract," or "to breach a duty."

**burden of proof** (noun). The duty to provide evidence which will support your case. In civil cases, the plaintiff has the burden of proof. In criminal cases, the prosecution has the burden of proof. The defense never has the burden of proof although it may have to rebut the plaintiff's case.

# C

**capital offense** (noun). A crime, such as murder, kidnapping or treason, which may be punishable by death in some jurisdictions.

**capital punishment** (noun). Death penalty, for capital offenses.

**cause of action** (noun). The facts which result in a lawsuit. When a lawsuit fails, it is determined that there was "no cause of action."

**certiorari** (Pronounced sir-shur-ARE-ee) (noun). Certification granted when the Supreme Court agrees to hear an appeal. Also known as "leave to appeal." As: The Supreme Court granted certiorari to only 50 cases last year."

**charge** (noun). A criminal accusation or criminal complaint.

**circumstantial evidence** (noun). Indirect evidence. Circumstantial evidence is generally admissible in court if it is relevant.

**citation** (noun). A reference to a specific law or case. As: "Can you give me the citation for that fact?" A summons to court issued for violation of a law or statute.

**civil action** (noun). Non-criminal case.

**civil law** (noun). Non-criminal law.

**civil rights** (noun). Rights granted by law to all people, to promote human dignity and social order.

**common law** (noun). Legal rules created on a case-by-case basis, which create a body of precedents which other courts tend to follow. Common law evolves over time based upon principles of justice, reason and common sense.

**compelling state interest** (noun). The overriding governmental necessity which must exist before the government is allowed to regulate or limit fundamental rights. (See *fundamental rights*.)

**compensation** (noun). Money or other valuables paid for: services rendered; damages caused; property taken.

**complainant** (noun). Plaintiff in a civil case or complaining witness in a criminal case. The complaining party.

**complaint** (noun). A legal document alleging crimes committed or civil damages caused to the complainant by the defendant. The document which, when accompanied by the summons, begins a lawsuit when served on the defendant.

**condemn** (verb). In criminal cases, to sentence one to death. To declare a property legally uninhabitable. A government act taking private property for public use under laws of eminent domain. (See *eminent domain*.)

**confess** (verb). To admit guilt.

**conspiracy** (noun). A criminal plan by two or more people acting together.

**Constitution** (noun). The document that embodies the supreme laws and principles of an organization or country.

**constitutional law** (noun). The branch of law concerned with interpreting the Constitution.

**contempt of court** (noun). Violation of a court order. Disobeying a judge or acting in a disrespectful way to a judge; punishable by fine or jail.

**contract** (noun). A legally binding agreement between parties for goods or services.

**convict** (verb). To find one guilty of a crime. (noun) A person found guilty of a crime.

**copyright** (noun). Exclusive rights granted by the government to artists, musicians and writers to control their works.

**counsel** (verb). To advise. (noun). An advisor or lawyer.

**court** (noun). A room or building in which legal cases are conducted. Sometimes used to refer to the legal authority of the judge. As: a ruling of the court.

**Court of Appeals** (See *appeals court*.)

**crime** (noun). An unlawful act for which punishment is imposed upon conviction.

**criminal** (noun). A person who commits a crime by an intentional or reckless act.

**cross-examination** (noun). Questions posed to a witness by opposing counsel during a trial or deposition, following direct examination.

**custody** (noun). A keeping or safeguarding. Control but not ownership.

# D

**damages** (noun). Legally recognized injuries. Monetary compensation paid for physical, emotional or economic injuries or for breach of contract. As: the court awarded him $1000 in damages.

**default** (verb). To lose a lawsuit by failing to respond.

**defamation of character** (noun). The injury to a person's reputation caused by passing on false statements about that person.

**defendant** (noun). The party who must defend against a criminal complaint or defend against a civil lawsuit.

**defense** (noun). A denial, explanation or answer to a criminal charge or civil lawsuit, denying responsibility or guilt.

**defraud** (verb). To damage another by lie, trick or misrepresentation.

**deposition** (noun). Out-of-court testimony of a witness made under oath, recorded by a court reporter and subject to examination by attorneys.

**direct examination** (noun). Questions asked to one's own witness during a deposition or trial. (See *cross-examination*.)

**discretion** (noun). The exercise of judicial power based on law, reason and experience. As: a judge must often exercise discretion while conducting a trial. Abuse of discretion by a judge or failing to exercise discretion may be grounds for reversal of a judge's ruling.

**dismiss** (verb). To end a lawsuit or criminal case before trial. A temporary dismissal is a "dismissal without prejudice." A permanent dismissal is called a "dismissal with prejudice."

**disorderly conduct** (noun). A crime involving loud, disturbing conduct such as fighting or public drunkenness. Also known as "disturbing the peace."

**divorce** (noun). The legal end to a marriage. (verb). To end a marriage.

**double jeopardy** (noun). Being subjected to trial more than once for the same crime. The guarantee against double jeopardy is part of the Fifth Amendment to the Constitution. Nonetheless, under some circumstances, people are put on trial for several different crimes arising out of the same act.

**due process of law** (noun). A constitutional civil right granted by the Fifth and Fourteenth Amendments that requires a fair hearing before one can be punished or deprived of liberty or property. The due process guarantees are some of the most important in the Constitution and are designed to guard against arbitrary and capricious behavior by government officials who might be tempted to abuse their authority. "Due process has not been reduced to any formula; its content cannot be determined by reference to any code. The best that can be said is that through the course of this court's decisions it has represented the balance which our nation, built upon postulates of respect for the liberty of the individual, has struck between that liberty and the demands of organized society." Justice Harlan, dissenting opinion in Griswold vs. Connecticut.

**duty** (noun). A legal obligation of one person to behave in a certain way to another.

# E

**emancipation** (noun). Freedom from bondage or slavery. Minors may be emancipated from their parents under some circumstances.

**eminent domain** (noun). The right of governments to purchase property for public use, even if the owner does not want to sell. (See *condemnation*.)

**equal protection of the law** (noun). Constitutional guarantee of equal treatment under law for people of all races, sexes, religions, national origins or incomes. A civil right stated in the Fourteenth Amendment which is designed to avoid arbitrary and capricious behavior on the part of government officials.

**equity** (noun). Justice. A branch of the legal system whose remedies include injunctions and other orders which require a party to do or refrain from doing specific acts. Today, courts of law and courts of equity are generally merged, but legal and equitable remedies are separate.

**equitable remedy** (noun). A remedy ordered by a court to cure an inequitable situation or injustice. Equitable remedies include injunctions, restraining orders, child custody orders, stays of enforcement and other orders requiring a party to act or refrain from acting.

**evidence** (noun). Proof. (See *admissible evidence*.)

**error** (noun). Mistakes made in court proceedings. "Reversible error," requires nullifying a judgment. "Harmless error," is not serious enough to cause such nullification.

**examination** (noun). Questions posed to a witness by an attorney in a trial or deposition.

**exclusionary rule** (noun). A rule which bars or excludes from use in trial any evidence that is improperly discovered by illegal police conduct.

**ex post facto laws** (noun). Latin, "after the fact." Laws which try to punish a person for behavior that was legal when it was done or increase the punishment. Such laws are prohibited by Article I of the U.S. Constitution.

**extenuating circumstances** (noun). Facts which reduce the guilt or responsibility of a person accused of a crime.

# F

**fair use** (noun). The exception to copyright which allows scholars and students to make limited use of copyrighted material without permission so long as it does not diminish the value of the copyright.

**false arrest** (noun). An unlawful arrest. A civil tort and/or a criminal act.

**false imprisonment** (noun). Unlawful detention or restraint of a person's freedom. A civil tort and/or criminal act.

**federal courts** (noun). Courts which enforce laws of the federal government of the United States. Federal courts also decide cases which involve parties from more than one state and cases between states.

**federalism** (noun). The system of government, as in the United States, where powers are shared between the individual states and a central government.

**felony** (noun). A serious criminal act, usually punishable by over one year in prison and/or fines. Called a "high misdemeanor" in some states.

**fighting words** (noun). Speech that incites violence in those who hear it.

**finding** (noun). A decision on the facts or law made by a judge or jury.

**fraud** (noun). An act which damages another by a lie, trick or misrepresentation. It may be a violation of criminal and/or civil law.

**freedom of speech** (noun). The right granted by the U.S. Constitution in the First Amendment giving people the right to openly express themselves without fear of retribution. The right is not unlimited, however, and may be regulated by the government as to time, manner and place. Defamatory and untrue speech may be punished by money damages awarded to the person who is defamed. "Fighting words" and "hate speech" which tend to inflame people to violence may also be prohibited.

**frisk** (verb). To pat down the outer clothes of a person in order to detect a gun or weapon. A frisk is not considered a search and is considered necessary under some circumstances to ensure the safety of police officers involved in criminal investigations.

**fundamental rights** (noun). Basic civil rights of U.S. citizens granted, recognized or implied by the Constitution which may not be taken away without due process of law and then only when there is an overriding governmental interest ("compelling state interest"). They include the rights to liberty, free speech, religion, privacy, the right to travel, to vote, to own property, to associate with whomever one wishes, to equal protection under law, to marry the person of one's choice. One person's liberty may be limited when it affects another person's health, safety or liberty.

# G

**grand jury** (noun). A group of citizens usually directed by a government prosecuting attorney who investigates facts and decides whether to seek criminal prosecutions ("indictments") against people suspected of criminal behavior. Grand juries have the power to subpoena witnesses who must testify under oath. (See *indictments*.)

**gross negligence** (noun). Heedless, willful and wanton negligence or conscious disregard of serious risk. More serious misconduct than ordinary negligence. Penalties for gross negligence exceed those for ordinary negligence and may include punitive (exemplary) damages.

**grounds** (noun). The underlying facts or justification for a case. The "cause of action."

**grounds for appeal** (noun). The reasons an appellant (person making the appeal) gives for requesting an appeal. Most common grounds for appeal are the following errors by the trial court: 1. improper jury instructions; 2. allowing improper evidence or testimony; 3. not allowing proper evidence or testimony; 4. remarks by the judge or attorney that prejudiced the jury and could not be corrected by an instruction; 5. misinterpreting the law; 6. discovery of important evidence that was not available at trial. (See *reversible error, appeal, appeals court*.)

**guilty** (adjective). Having committed a crime proven either by admission or determined by a judge or jury.

# H

**hearing** (noun). A legal proceeding to hear facts and evidence and render a decision. A hearing may be conducted by a judge, or in school settings by school officials. Many hearings do not have the same strict rules of evidence and procedure required in court.

**hearsay** (noun). Statement made outside court in which one person tells what someone else supposedly said. Usually not admissible in evidence at trial because of its unreliable nature. Hearsay is admissible in some hearings, including public school disciplinary hearings.

**homicide** (noun). Any killing, whether lawful or unlawful, of one person by another (See *murder*.)

**hung jury** (noun). A jury which is unable to reach a verdict because its members cannot agree. The result of a hung jury is a mistrial which may result in a retrial or occasionally result in a dismissal.

# I

**indictment** (pronounced in-DITE-ment) (noun). A written accusation prepared by a prosecutor and endorsed by a grand jury formally accusing a person of criminal wrongdoing and specifying the crime with enough specificity to allow the accused to prepare a defense.

**infraction** (noun). A violation of a law, rule or regulation.

**injunction** (noun). A court order which prohibits a person or organization from doing a certain act. An injunction is designed to protect and prevent irreparable harm. Injunctions are known as "equitable" relief.

**in re** (Latin). "in the matter of." Regarding.

**intent** (noun). The state of mind which is necessary for a wrongful act to be criminal. Some crimes require "specific intent." Other crimes have a lower standard requiring only "general intent" as shown by reckless behavior or willful and wanton behavior.

**intentional tort** (noun). A wrongful act committed intentionally. Assault and battery and fraud are two intentional torts. Damages awarded for intentional acts are often greater than damages awarded for ordinary negligence.

**irrelevant** (adjective). Not related to the case and therefore inadmissible as evidence.

# J

**judge** (noun). A public official either appointed or elected who hears and decides cases. Most states require judges to be practicing attorneys.

**judgment** (noun). The decision made by a judge or jury after a trial.

**jurisdiction** (noun). The authority to hear and decide a case. As in: family court has no jurisdiction over a traffic ticket. The location in which a law applies.

**jurist** (noun). A legal scholar or judge.

**juror** (noun). A member of a jury.

**jury** (noun). A group of citizens of legal age drawn from the community who hear and decide the facts of a trial and render a verdict based on the law as told to them by the judge.

**juvenile court** (noun). A court with sole jurisdiction over minors. Some accused criminals under 18 years of age may be tried as adults outside juvenile court.

**juvenile delinquent** (noun). A minor convicted of a crime.

# L

**larceny** (noun). Theft. Taking the property of another without permission, with the intent to permanently deprive the owner of its use or possession.

**law** (noun). A rule of conduct intended to maintain order and benefit the public welfare.

**lawsuit** (noun). A civil action filed in court by a plaintiff asking the court to award the plaintiff money damages or other relief as a remedy for injuries allegedly caused by the defendant.

**lawyer** (noun). A person licensed to practice law.

**legislation** (noun). A law or rule proposed or passed by a legislature which may include penalties and prescribe compensation. (verb). The act of lawmaking by legislators in a legislative body.

**legislature** (noun). A group of people elected by citizens to enact laws and rules for their jurisdiction.

**liable** (adjective). Legally responsible.

**liability** (noun). Responsibility; either criminal, civil, financial or equitable. A legal duty to act or pay for damages. A debt owed.

**libel** (noun). A false or misleading publication which tends to harm a person's reputation. (See also *slander, defamation of character*.)

**liberty** (noun). The freedom of activity granted by the Constitution and limited by laws only when its exercise interferes with the rights of others.

**license** (noun). Officially granted permission to engage in a legally restricted activity such as architect, builder, doctor, lawyer, nurse, electrician, plumber, pharmacist, teacher, driver, etc.

**litigation** (noun). Lawsuits; legal action in court.

# M

**majority, age of** (noun). The age at which one becomes a legal adult, responsible for his or her own affairs, contracts and obligations. Age at which a person becomes eligible to vote in the United States (18 years of age, pursuant to the Twenty-Sixth Amendment passed in 1972).

**malice** (noun). The intent to cause harm to others without justification.

**manslaughter** (noun). A criminal homicide caused not with "malice" but by extreme recklessness or criminal negligence. The killing of a person caused by the gross misconduct by a person who engaged in an activity with unnecessarily high risk such as drunk driving or reckless discharge of a firearm.

**mediation** (noun). A process in which parties to a disagreement meet with a mediator and discuss and attempt to resolve their problem.

**mediator** (noun). A person trained or skilled in the process of conducting mediation and resolving conflicts. A negotiator.

**minor** (noun). A person who has not yet reached the age of majority, i.e. legal adulthood.

**miranda warnings** (noun). Warnings which must be given to criminal suspects after arrest, advising them of their right to remain silent and to consult an attorney. Named after the U.S. Supreme Court case, Miranda vs. Arizona.

**misdemeanor** (noun). A minor crime usually punishable by less than one year in jail and/or a fine.

**mistrial** (noun). A trial which is terminated before a decision because of a problem which cannot be remedied. Mistrial may result when an improper piece of evidence is seen by a jury or improper arguments are made by a lawyer and the judge decides that the impropriety cannot be cured by corrective jury instructions. (See also *hung jury*.)

**motion** (noun). A request to the court for an order, ruling or judgment by a party in a civil lawsuit or criminal trial.

**murder** (noun). Unlawful killing of a person. First degree murder is committed intentionally, with malice and premeditation (planning). Second degree murder is done intentionally, with malice, but without premeditation. Penalties are more severe for first degree murder. (See also *manslaughter*.)

# N

**negligence** (noun). Carelessness. Breach of the "duty of care" expected of reasonable people.

**notice** (noun). Legal notification of a legal action. The law requires that a person be informed of a pending legal action in which he or she is named as a party before the court can act against him or her. (See *service of process*.)

**notary public** (noun). A person authorized by law to validate signatures and affidavits.

**nuisance** (noun). Anything which disturbs, annoys or interferes with the rights of a property owner to peaceful enjoyment of his property. A tort may be created by noise, odor, vibration, pollution, smoke, etc.

# O

**offer** (noun). In contracts, a promise which invites acceptance and, if accepted in a timely fashion, creates a contract.

**opinion** (noun). The reasons justifying the decision in the case.

**order** (noun). A command issued by a judge, having the force of law.

**ordinance** (noun). A local law. As: a city ordinance.

# P

**party** (noun). A person directly involved. In a lawsuit, either plaintiff or defendant. In a contract, a person who is a signer.

**patent** (noun). An exclusive right granted by the government to inventors to use, sell, manufacture or license their invention for 17 years.

**perjury** (noun). The crime of making false statements under oath.

**per se** (Latin) (adjective). "by itself." Having an intrinsic characteristic. For example, if a driver runs a stop sign and causes an accident, he is negligent, *per se.*

**plaintiff** (noun). The party that brings a lawsuit against the defendant. (See also *complainant.*)

**plead** (verb). To make a legal answer or argument. As: to plead "guilty" or "not guilty."

**pleadings** (noun). The legal papers of a lawsuit, specifically the Complaint and Answer to Complaint.

**police power** (noun). The constitutional authority granted to government to make and enforce regulations and laws reasonably related to protection of public health and safety.

**power of attorney** (noun). The appointment of a person to act in one's place when one is unable to act for oneself.

**precedent** (noun). A previously decided case used as authority in later cases on a similar subject. Lower courts must follow precedents set by higher courts in the same jurisdiction. (See *res judicata.*)

**preponderance of the evidence** (noun). The standard of proof required to win most civil cases. To win a civil case, plaintiff must do so by at least 51% of the evidence to tip the "scales of justice," in their favor.

**privacy** (noun). "The right to be left alone." A fundamental right as defined by Supreme Court decisions but distinguished from many fundamental rights in that it is not explicitly listed in the Constitution or Bill of Rights. Other fundamental rights not specifically listed are the right to bear children, the right to associate freely and the right to travel freely. It is argued that such freedoms, including privacy, are created in the "penumbra" (or partial shadow between two objects) between several other explicitly listed, constitutionally guaranteed freedoms. The have also been called among "the basic civil rights of man" in Skinner vs. Oklahoma

**protected speech** (noun). Any form of speech which is protected by the Constitution. Political speech is generally one of the forms of free speech receiving the highest level of protection.

**proximate cause** (noun). Direct or actual cause of a plaintiff's injury.

**prima facie** (Latin) (adjective). "On first view," or "on its face." The basic showing of proof required to win a case.

**probable cause** (noun). Before a judge may issue a search warrant or arrest warrant, there must exist a reasonable suspicion ("probable cause") based on legitimate information that the person to be arrested has committed a crime or that the place to be searched contains the evidence sought. Probable cause is also required before a police officer may arrest and search a suspect without a warrant. The officer or judge must have probable cause to believe that a crime has been committed and that the suspect committed it. (See the Fourth Amendment to the Constitution.)

**probation** (noun). Conditions of sentencing set by a judge as an alternative to sending a person convicted of a crime to jail.

**proof** (noun). Evidence required to establish or prove an allegation.

**prosecute** (verb). To pursue a lawsuit or, in criminal law, to seek a criminal conviction. Only a government attorney may prosecute a criminal case.

**prosecutor** (noun). Also prosecuting attorney or district attorney. The public official whose job is to prosecute those accused of crimes. Prosecutors must use their discretion to determine which acts appear to be crimes and when there is enough evidence to charge a person with a crime.

**public domain** (noun). Public property, owned by all equally, as opposed to private property. Intellectual property such as inventions, writings and artworks, is considered to be in the public domain if it is not protected by patent, copyright or trademark.

**punitive damages** (noun). Damages that exceed the pure dollar loss suffered by a plaintiff. Punitive damages are assessed if a judge or jury decides that a defendant acted intentionally or with gross negligence. Punitive damages are designed to punish and deter wrongdoing.

# Q

**quid pro quo** (Latin phrase). "Something for something." The exchange of things of value in a contract.

**quiet enjoyment** (noun). The right of a property owner to undisturbed use of his or her lands.

# R

**reasonable** (noun). Fair, moderate; within the bounds of common sense. (See *beyond a reasonable doubt*.)

**reasonableness** (noun). A legal standard which assumes an average amount of intelligence and care exercised by the so called "reasonable person."

**reasonable person** (noun). A legal standard which assumes that the average person should behave in a prudent manner. Juries are allowed to decide how a reasonable person would act in a given situation and judge a party to a lawsuit accordingly. *Negligence* is often defined as "a breach of the duty of care that would be expected from a reasonable person."

**recess** (noun). A temporary adjournment or break in a trial.

**reckless** (adjective). Heedless, wanton. Conscious disregard of the consequences of one's acts.

**regulation** (noun). A rule which has the power of law but is made by unelected regulators using the authority granted them by elected officials.

**relevant** (adjective). Appropriate to prove a matter before the court. Evidence must be relevant to be admissible.

**remedy** (noun). The tools that a court uses to compensate a plaintiff who proves his or her case. Money is the most common remedy. Injunctions, restraining orders or other "equitable" remedies are granted in cases where money alone will not provide an "adequate remedy at law." (See *equity*.)

**res ipsa loquitur** (Latin phrase). "The thing speaks for itself." The doctrine that negligence may be inferred in some circumstances when: an injury would have been unlikely to have happened in the absence of negligence and; the causing of the injury is in the exclusive control of the defendant.

**res judicata** (Latin phrase). "Already decided."

**restitution** (noun). Compensation for monetary loss. Criminal defendants are often ordered to pay restitution to their victims.

**restraining order** (noun). A permanent or temporary injunction ordering a halt to some action. A temporary restraining order (TRO) is valid until there is a complete hearing on the matter. Designed to stop irreparable damage that may occur before a full hearing can be held, such as chopping down trees, tearing down a building or harassing a former spouse.

**reverse** (verb). To overturn or overrule. As: an appeals court may reverse the decision of a trial court.

**reversible error** (noun). A mistake committed during a trial or proceeding that is so serious as to require that the court's ruling or verdict be overturned.

**robbery** (noun). Larceny from a person by force or threat of force.

**rule** (noun). A principle of law or procedure.

**ruling** (noun). A decision by a judge on a point of law or procedure.

# S

**search warrant** (noun). A court order required by the Fourth Amendment before police can enter and search a home or a person. It must specify the place to be searched and specific objects sought and cannot be issued unless the judge is convinced that there is probable cause. (See *probable cause*.) The requirement is designed to prohibit unreasonable searches and seizures by police or government officials. Private parties such as parents are not required to obtain search warrants. However, improper searches by private individuals may be considered invasions of privacy which have civil remedies.

**self-defense** (noun). The right to protect oneself or others from imminent attack. To be a valid defense to a charge of assault and battery, the force used must not exceed the amount necessary to repel the attack; the person using it must not be guilty of provoking or starting the fight and, in some states, there must have been no opportunity to retreat easily to a place of safety.

**segregation** (noun). Physical separation of people, usually by race.

**sentence** (noun). The punishment ordered by a court for one convicted of a crime. It may consist of a fine and/or imprisonment, restitution to the victim or probation.

**service of process** (noun). Delivery of a legal document to a party in a lawsuit. A lawsuit commences when the defendant is personally served with a complaint and summons to court.

**settlement** (noun). An agreement between the parties to resolve a lawsuit before trial.

**slander** (noun). A false oral statement which defames or harms a person's reputation. (See *libel* and *defamation of character*.)

**standard** (noun). Criterion or bench mark.

**standing** (noun). The right or capacity to initiate a lawsuit regarding a law or action which affects one directly. Only those people with enough direct stake in a case have "standing" to file a lawsuit. Because courts have authority to resolve only disputes which involve actual harm, legal actions cannot be brought simply on the grounds a party is unhappy with a law.

**state courts** (noun). Courts which administer the laws of a state. State courts may also rule on U.S. constitutional issues.

**statute** (noun). A law enacted by a legislature.

**statute of limitations** (noun). The law that limits the time in which a suit can be filed. Also known as the "limitation on actions."

**stay** (noun). A court order temporarily suspending a proceeding until a specific event has occurred.

**strict liability** (noun). A legal doctrine in which persons (or companies) who engage in certain activities are held accountable for all damages they cause whether or not they are negligent. For example, a manufacturer who makes a faulty product is liable for injuries it causes even if he did not know the product was faulty.

**subpoena** (noun). An order to a witness to appear before the court, issued by a judge or court officer. The U.S. Congress also has the power to subpoena any citizen of the United States to appear and testify before it under oath. Congressional investigations and hearings play an integral part of governmental decision making. Abuse of such power is an abuse of discretion. The McCarthy Hearings of the 1950s are the classic example of congressional subpoena power run amok.

**summons** (noun). A court order requiring a party to appear in court.

**sue** (verb). To file a civil lawsuit in court.

**suit** (noun). A proceeding in court to recover a right or claim. (See *lawsuit*.)

**supreme court** (noun). The highest court of a state or of the United States. The United States Supreme Court and lower courts are created by the Constitution. Rulings by the U.S. Supreme Court may not be overruled by any other U.S. court.

**suspect** (noun). A person suspected of, but not yet charged with, committing a crime.

# T

**testimony** (noun). Statements made in court under oath by a witness and used as evidence.

**tort** (noun). A wrong. An injury to one person directly caused by another. A class of legal action whose elements are: a legal duty owed by one person to another; a breach of that duty; injury directly (proximately) caused by the breach. A court can award compensation to be paid by the defendant to the plaintiff in an attempt to right the wrong.

**tort-feasor** (noun). Wrongdoer.

**trademark** (noun). A word, symbol or brand name used to identify and distinguish one product from another.

**trespass** (noun). A wrongful interference with or invasion of the property of another.

**trial** (noun). The conduct of a civil lawsuit or criminal proceeding in which blame or guilt is determined.

**truancy** (noun). The unlawful absence from school.

# U

**unconstitutional** (adjective). An act or law which violates the Constitution and is therefore void and unenforceable.

# V

**valid** (adjective). Legal, lawful and proper.

**verdict** (noun). The final decision of a judge or jury in a civil lawsuit or criminal trial.

**void** (adjective). Having no legal force. As if it never existed.

**void for vagueness** (adjective). A law is void and unconstitutional if it is so vague that a reasonable person would not know what acts the law made illegal.

**voir dire** (French, pronounced "vwar deer") (noun). Examination by attorney or judge of prospective jurors or witnesses conducted to see if they are qualified, unbiased and truthful.

# W

**warrant** (noun). A written arrest authorization issued by a judge.

**will** (noun). A legal document which a person writes indicating how he or she desires to have his or her possessions distributed after death.

**witness** (noun). One who testifies in court, under oath, to facts he or she knows or events which he or she personally saw. Also a person who watches as someone signs an official document.

# Selected Online Resources

*Rather than supply a standard bibliography,*
*it seems more useful to include a list of legal resource web sites.*

## General Legal Resources

**The American Civil Liberties Homepage**
http://www.aclu.org An excellent site for civil rights and civil liberties information.

**The American Library Association Homepage**
http://www.ala.org/ is an excellent site regarding freedom of speech and Banned Books Week.

**Cleveland Marshall School of Law,**
**Law Library**
http://www.law.csuohio.edu/lawlibrary/
An excellent source of general legal information and links.

**Cornell University, Law Library**
http://www.lawschool.cornell.edu/lawlibrary/

**FindLaw.com**
http://www.findlaw.com/
A good general law site and especially good for finding U.S. Supreme Court decisions. Finding specific cases is easier if you have the exact "U.S. Reports" citation already. The first number in the string is the volume number. The second is the page number. For example: Goss vs. Lopez, 419 U.S. 565, (1975) is cited in FindLaw as: http://www.laws.findlaw.com/us/419/565.html

**The Freedom Forum Homepage**
http://www.freedomforum.org

**Galt Union School District Drug Dog Lawsuit**
http://www.softcom.net/users/kareed/
This is an excellent site regarding students' rights.

**Law News Network** http://www.lawnewsnetwork.com/
An on-line periodical of legal news.

**Laws.com**
http://www.laws.com/
A compendium of legal resources from the U.S. and Canada.

**Mediation**
http://www.law.csuohio.edu/
If you are interested in more information on setting up a peer mediation program in your school, you can also write: Cleveland Marshall School of Law, 1801 Euclid Avenue, Cleveland, Ohio 44115 or phone: (216) 687-2250.

**National Association of Attorneys General**
http://www.naag.org/
Here is the online newsletter of the top law enforcement officials of all the states in the U.S.

**The U.S. Constitution**
http://www.house.gov/Constitution/Constitution.html
Online from the the House of Representatives' web site.

**U.S. Constitution**
http://www.nara.gov/exhall/charters/constitution/conmain.html From the National Archives and Records Administration.

**United States Government Office of Copyrights**
http://lcweb.loc.gov/copyright/

**United States Government Patent and Trademark Office**
http://www.uspto.gov/

# Caselaw Citations

**Board of Education, Island Trees Union Free School District No. 26 vs. Pico,** 457 U.S. 853 (1982) at http://laws.findlaw.com/us/457/853.html. Book banning in schools.

**Brown vs. Board of Education of Topeka,** 349 U.S. 294 (1955) at http://laws.findlaw.com/us/349/294.html Racial segregation of public schools.

**Goss vs. Lopez,** 419 U.S. 565 (1975) at http://laws.find-law.com/us/419/565.html1975 Still the standard on student rights regarding suspension and expulsion.

**Hazelwood School District vs. Kuhlmeier** 484 U.S. 260 (1988) at http://laws.findlaw.com/us/484/260.html School newspaper censorship.

**Korematsu vs. United States,** 323 U.S. 214 (1944) at http://laws.findlaw.com/us/323/214 Japanese relocation during WWII.

**New Jersey vs. T.L.O.,** 468 U.S. 1214 (1984) at http://laws.findlaw.com/us/468/1214.html Set the standard for searching students in schools.

**New York Times vs. Sullivan** 376 U.S. 255 (1964) at http://laws.findlaw.com/us/376/255.html Libel standard regarding public figures.

**Tinker vs. Des Moines School District** 393 U.S. 503 (1969) at http://laws.findlaw.com/us/393/503.html Freedom of speech.

**Veronia School District 47J vs. Acton** (94-590), 515 U.S. 646 (1995) at http://laws.findlaw.com/US/000/U10263.html Random drug testing of student athletes.

# Newspaper Articles

**Drug Testing in Veronia High School** http://www.seattletimes.com/extra/browse/html/drug_103196.html

# The United States Constitution

*With original spelling, punctuation and capitalization*

**WE THE PEOPLE** of the United States, in Order to form a more perfect Union, establish Justice, insure domestic Tranquility, provide for the common defence, promote the general Welfare, and secure the Blessings of Liberty to ourselves and our Posterity, do ordain and establish this Constitution for the United States of America.

## ARTICLE I

## SECTION 1

All legislative Powers herein granted shall be vested in a Congress of the United States, which shall consist of a Senate and House of Representatives.

## SECTION 2

The House of Representatives shall be composed of Members chosen every second Year by the People of the several States, and the Electors in each State shall have the Qualifications requisite for Electors of the most numerous Branch of the State Legislature.

No Person shall be a Representative who shall not have attained to the Age of twenty five Years, and been seven Years a Citizen of the United States, and who shall not, when elected, be an Inhabitant of that State in which he shall be chosen.

Representatives and direct Taxes shall be apportioned among the several States which may be included within this Union, according to their respective Numbers, which shall be determined by adding to the whole Number of free Persons, including those bound to Service for a Term of Years, and excluding Indians not taxed, three fifths of all other Persons. The actual Enumeration shall be made within three Years after the first Meeting of the Congress of the United States, and within every subsequent Term of ten Years, in such Manner as they shall by Law direct. The Number of Representatives shall not exceed one for every thirty Thousand, but each State shall have at Least one Representative; and until such enumeration shall be made, the State of New Hampshire shall be entitled to chuse three, Massachusetts eight, Rhode-Island and Providence Plantations one, Connecticut five, New-York six, New Jersey four, Pennsylvania eight, Delaware one, Maryland six, Virginia ten, North Carolina five, South Carolina five, and Georgia three.

When vacancies happen in the Representation from any State, the Executive Authority thereof shall issue Writs of Election to fill such Vacancies.

The House of Representatives shall chuse their Speaker and other Officers; and shall have the sole Power of Impeachment.

## SECTION 3

The Senate of the United States shall be composed of two Senators from each State, chosen by the Legislature thereof, for six Years; and each Senator shall have one Vote.

Immediately after they shall be assembled in Consequence of the first Election, they shall be divided as equally as may be into three Classes. The Seats of the Senators of the first Class shall be vacated at the Expiration of the second Year, of the second Class at the Expiration of the fourth Year, and of the third Class at the Expiration of the sixth Year, so that one third may be chosen every second Year; and if Vacancies happen by Resignation, or otherwise, during the Recess of the Legislature of any State, the Executive thereof may make temporary Appointments until the next Meeting of the Legislature, which shall then fill such Vacancies.

No Person shall be a Senator who shall not have attained to the Age of thirty Years, and been nine Years a Citizen of the United States, and who shall not, when elected, be an Inhabitant of that State for which he shall be chosen.

The Vice President of the United States shall be President of the Senate, but shall have no Vote, unless they be equally divided.

The Senate shall chuse their other Officers, and also a President pro tempore, in the Absence of the Vice President, or when he shall exercise the Office of President of the United States.

The Senate shall have the sole Power to try all Impeachments. When sitting for that Purpose, they shall be on Oath or Affirmation. When the President of the United States is tried, the Chief Justice shall preside: And no Person shall be convicted without the Concurrence of two thirds of the Members present.

Judgment in Cases of Impeachment shall not extend further than to removal from Office, and disqualification to hold and enjoy any Office of honor, Trust or Profit under the United States: but the Party convicted shall nevertheless be liable and subject to Indictment, Trial, Judgment and Punishment, according to Law.

## SECTION 4

The Times, Places and Manner of holding Elections for Senators and Representatives, shall be prescribed in each State by the Legislature thereof; but the Congress may at any time by Law make or alter such Regulations, except as to the Places of chusing Senators.

The Congress shall assemble at least once in every Year, and such Meeting shall be on the first Monday in December, unless they shall by Law appoint a different Day.

## SECTION 5

Each House shall be the Judge of the Elections, Returns and Qualifications of its own Members, and a Majority of each shall constitute a Quorum to do Business; but a smaller Number may adjourn from day to day, and may be authorized to compel the Attendance of absent Members, in such Manner, and under such Penalties as each House may provide.

Each House may determine the Rules of its Proceedings, punish its Members for disorderly Behaviour, and, with the Concurrence of two thirds, expel a Member.

Each House shall keep a Journal of its Proceedings, and from time to time publish the same, excepting such Parts as may in their Judgment require Secrecy; and the Yeas and Nays of the Members of either House on any question shall, at the Desire of one fifth of those Present, be entered on the Journal.

Neither House, during the Session of Congress, shall, without the Consent of the other, adjourn for more than three days, nor to any other Place than that in which the two Houses shall be sitting.

## SECTION 6

The Senators and Representatives shall receive a Compensation for their Services, to be ascertained by Law, and paid out of the Treasury of the United States. They shall in all Cases, except Treason, Felony and Breach of the Peace, be privileged from Arrest during their Attendance at the Session of their respective Houses, and in going to and returning from the same; and for any Speech or Debate in either House, they shall not be questioned in any other Place.

No Senator or Representative shall, during the Time for which he was elected, be appointed to any civil Office under the Authority of the United States, which shall have been created, or the Emoluments whereof shall have been encreased during such time; and no Person holding any Office under the United States, shall be a Member of either House during his Continuance in Office.

# SECTION 7

All Bills for raising Revenue shall originate in the House of Representatives; but the Senate may propose or concur with Amendments as on other Bills.

Every Bill which shall have passed the House of Representatives and the Senate, shall, before it become a Law, be presented to the President of the United States; If he approve he shall sign it, but if not he shall return it, with his Objections to that House in which it shall have originated, who shall enter the Objections at large on their Journal, and proceed to reconsider it. If after such Reconsideration two thirds of that House shall agree to pass the Bill, it shall be sent, together with the Objections, to the other House, by which it shall likewise be reconsidered, and if approved by two thirds of that House, it shall become a Law. But in all such Cases the Votes of both Houses shall be determined by yeas and Nays, and the Names of the persons voting for and against the Bill shall be entered on the Journal of each House respectively. If any Bill shall not be returned by the President within ten Days (Sundays excepted) after it shall have been presented to him, the Same shall be a Law, in like Manner as if he had signed it, unless the Congress by their Adjournment prevent its Return, in which Case it shall not be a Law.

Every Order, Resolution, or Vote to which the Concurrence of the Senate and House of Representatives may be necessary (except on a question of Adjournment) shall be presented to the President of the United States; and before the Same shall take Effect, shall be approved by him, or being disapproved by him, shall be repassed by two thirds of the Senate and House of Representatives, according to the Rules and Limitations prescribed in the Case of a Bill.

# SECTION 8

The Congress shall have Power To lay and collect Taxes, Duties, Imposts and Excises, to pay the Debts and provide for the common Defence and general Welfare of the United States; but all Duties, Imposts and Excises shall be uniform throughout the United States;

To borrow Money on the credit of the United States;

To regulate Commerce with foreign Nations, and among the several States, and with the Indian Tribes;

To establish an uniform Rule of Naturalization, and uniform Laws on the subject of Bankruptcies throughout the United States;

To coin Money, regulate the Value thereof, and of foreign Coin, and fix the Standard of Weights and Measures;

To provide for the Punishment of counterfeiting the Securities and current Coin of the United States;

To establish Post Offices and post Roads;

To promote the Progress of Science and useful Arts, by securing for limited Times to Authors and Inventors the exclusive Right to their respective Writings and Discoveries;

To constitute Tribunals inferior to the supreme Court;

To define and punish Piracies and Felonies committed on the high Seas, and Offences against the Law of Nations;

To declare War, grant Letters of Marque and Reprisal, and make Rules concerning Captures on Land and Water;

To raise and support Armies, but no Appropriation of Money to that Use shall be for a longer Term than two Years;

To provide and maintain a Navy;

To make Rules for the Government and Regulation of the land and naval Forces; To provide for calling forth the Militia to execute the Laws of the Union, suppress Insurrections and repel Invasions;

To provide for organizing, arming, and disciplining, the Militia, and for governing such Part of them as may be employed in the Service of the United States, reserving to the States respectively, the Appointment of the Officers, and the Authority of training the Militia according to the discipline prescribed by Congress;

To exercise exclusive Legislation in all Cases whatsoever, over such District (not exceeding ten Miles square) as may, by Cession of particular States, and the Acceptance of Congress, become the Seat of the Government of the United States, and to exercise like Authority over all Places purchased by the Consent of the Legislature of the State in which the Same shall be, for the Erection of Forts, Magazines, Arsenals, dock-Yards, and other needful Buildings;—And to make all Laws which shall be necessary and proper for carrying into Execution the foregoing Powers, and all other Powers vested by this Constitution in the Government of the United States, or in any Department or Officer thereof.

## SECTION 9

The Migration or Importation of such Persons as any of the States now existing shall think proper to admit, shall not be prohibited by the Congress prior to the Year one thousand eight hundred and eight, but a Tax or duty may be imposed on such Importation, not exceeding ten dollars for each Person.

The Privilege of the Writ of Habeas Corpus shall not be suspended, unless when in Cases of Rebellion or Invasion the public Safety may require it.

No Bill of Attainder or ex post facto Law shall be passed.

No Capitation, or other direct, Tax shall be laid, unless in Proportion to the Census or Enumeration herein before directed to be taken.

No Tax or Duty shall be laid on Articles exported from any State.

No Preference shall be given by any Regulation of Commerce or Revenue to the Ports of one State over those of another: nor shall Vessels bound to, or from, one State, be obliged to enter, clear, or pay Duties in another.

No Money shall be drawn from the Treasury, but in Consequence of Appropriations made by Law; and a regular Statement and Account of the Receipts and Expenditures of all public Money shall be published from time to time.

No Title of Nobility shall be granted by the United States: And no Person holding any Office of Profit or Trust under them, shall, without the Consent of the Congress, accept of any present, Emolument, Office, or Title, of any kind whatever, from any King, Prince, or foreign State.

# SECTION 10

No State shall enter into any Treaty, Alliance, or Confederation; grant Letters of Marque and Reprisal; coin Money; emit Bills of Credit; make any Thing but gold and silver Coin a Tender in Payment of Debts; pass any Bill of Attainder, ex post facto Law, or Law impairing the Obligation of Contracts, or grant any Title of Nobility.

No State shall, without the Consent of the Congress, lay any Imposts or Duties on Imports or Exports, except what may be absolutely necessary for executing its inspection Laws: and the net Produce of all Duties and Imposts, laid by any State on Imports or Exports, shall be for the Use of the Treasury of the United States; and all such Laws shall be subject to the Revision and Controul of the Congress.

No State shall, without the Consent of Congress, lay any Duty of Tonnage, keep Troops, or Ships of War in time of Peace, enter into any Agreement or Compact with another State, or with a foreign Power, or engage in War, unless actually invaded, or in such imminent Danger as will not admit of delay.

# ARTICLE II

## SECTION 1

The executive Power shall be vested in a President of the United States of America. He shall hold his Office during the Term of four Years, and, together with the Vice President, chosen for the same Term, be elected, as follows.

Each State shall appoint, in such Manner as the Legislature thereof may direct, a Number of Electors, equal to the whole Number of Senators and Representatives to which the State may be entitled in the Congress:  but no Senator or Representative, or Person holding an Office of Trust or Profit under the United States, shall be appointed an Elector.

The Electors shall meet in their respective States, and vote by Ballot for two Persons, of whom one at least shall not be an Inhabitant of the same State with themselves. And they shall make a List of all the Persons voted for, and of the Number of Votes for each; which List they shall sign and certify, and transmit sealed to the Seat of the Government of the United States, directed to the President of the Senate. The President of the Senate shall, in the Presence of the Senate and House of Representatives, open all the Certificates, and the Votes shall then be counted. The Person having the greatest Number of Votes shall be the President, if such Number be a Majority of the whole Number of Electors appointed; and if there be more than one who have such Majority, and have an equal Number of Votes, then the House of Representatives shall immediately chuse by Ballot one of them for President; and if no Person have a Majority, then from the five highest on the List the said House shall in like Manner chuse the President. But in chusing the President, the Votes shall be taken by States, the Representation from each State having one Vote; A quorum for this Purpose shall consist of a Member or Members from two thirds of the States, and a Majority of all the States shall be necessary to a Choice. In every Case, after the Choice of the President, the Person having the greatest Number of Votes of the Electors shall be the Vice President. But if there should remain two or more who have equal Votes, the Senate shall chuse from them by Ballot the Vice President.

The Congress may determine the Time of chusing the Electors, and the Day on which they shall give their Votes; which Day shall be the same throughout the United States.

No Person except a natural born Citizen, or a Citizen of the United States, at the time of the Adoption of this Constitution, shall be eligible to the Office of President; neither shall any Person be eligible to that Office who shall not have attained to the Age of thirty five Years, and been fourteen Years a Resident within the United States.

In Case of the Removal of the President from Office, or of his Death, Resignation, or Inability to discharge the Powers and Duties of the said Office, the Same shall devolve on the Vice President, and the Congress may by Law provide for the Case of Removal, Death, Resignation or Inability, both of the President and Vice President, declaring what Officer shall then act as President, and such Officer shall act accordingly, until the Disability be removed, or a President shall be elected.

The President shall, at stated Times, receive for his Services, a Compensation, which shall neither be encreased nor diminished during the Period for which he shall have been elected, and he shall not receive within that Period any other Emolument from the United States, or any of them.

Before he enter on the Execution of his Office, he shall take the following Oath or Affirmation–"I do solemnly swear (or affirm) that I will faithfully execute the Office of President of the United States, and will to the best of my Ability, preserve, protect and defend the Constitution of the United States."

TLC10242 Copyright © Teaching & Learning Company, Carthage, IL 62321-0010

# SECTION 2

The President shall be Commander in Chief of the Army and Navy of the United States, and of the Militia of the several States, when called into the actual Service of the United States; he may require the Opinion, in writing, of the principal Officer in each of the executive Departments, upon any Subject relating to the Duties of their respective Offices, and he shall have Power to grant Reprieves and Pardons for Offences against the United States, except in Cases of Impeachment.

He shall have Power, by and with the Advice and Consent of the Senate, to make Treaties, provided two thirds of the Senators present concur; and he shall nominate, and by and with the Advice and Consent of the Senate, shall appoint Ambassadors, other public Ministers and Consuls, Judges of the supreme Court, and all other Officers of the United States, whose Appointments are not herein otherwise provided for, and which shall be established by Law: but the Congress may by Law vest the Appointment of such inferior Officers, as they think proper, in the President alone, in the Courts of Law, or in the Heads of Departments.

The President shall have Power to fill up all Vacancies that may happen during the Recess of the Senate, by granting Commissions which shall expire at the End of their next Session.

# SECTION 3

He shall from time to time give to the Congress Information of the State of the Union, and recommend to their Consideration such Measures as he shall judge necessary and expedient; he may on extraordinary Occasions, convene both Houses, or either of them, and in Case of Disagreement between them, with Respect to the Time of Adjournment, he may adjourn them to such Time as he shall think proper; he shall receive Ambassadors and other public Ministers; he shall take Care that the Laws be faithfully executed, and shall Commission all the Officers of the United States.

## SECTION 4

The President, Vice President and all civil Officers of the United States, shall be removed from Office on Impeachment for, and Conviction of, Treason, Bribery, or other high Crimes and Misdemeanors

## ARTICLE III

## SECTION 1

The judicial Power of the United States, shall be vested in one supreme Court, and in such inferior Courts as the Congress may from time to time ordain and establish. The Judges, both of the supreme and inferior Courts, shall hold their Offices during good Behaviour, and shall, at stated Times, receive for their Services, a Compensation, which shall not be diminished during their Continuance in Office.

## SECTION 2

The judicial Power shall extend to all Cases, in Law and Equity, arising under this Constitution, the Laws of the United States, and Treaties made, or which shall be made, under their Authority;—to all Cases affecting Ambassadors, other public Ministers and Consuls;—to all Cases of admiralty and maritime Jurisdiction;—to Controversies to which the United States shall be a Party;—to Controversies between two or more States;—between a State and Citizens of another State;—between Citizens of different States,—between Citizens of the same State claiming Lands under Grants of different States, and between a State, or the Citizens thereof, and foreign States, Citizens or Subjects.

In all Cases affecting Ambassadors, other public Ministers and Consuls, and those in which a State shall be Party, the supreme Court shall have original Jurisdiction. In all the other Cases before mentioned, the supreme Court shall have appellate Jurisdiction, both as to Law and Fact, with such Exceptions, and under such Regulations as the Congress shall make.

The Trial of all Crimes, except in Cases of Impeachment, shall be by Jury; and such Trial shall be held in the State where the said Crimes shall have been committed; but when not committed within any State, the Trial shall be at such Place or Places as the Congress may by Law have directed.

## SECTION 3

Treason against the United States, shall consist only in levying War against them, or in adhering to their Enemies, giving them Aid and Comfort. No Person shall be convicted of Treason unless on the Testimony of two Witnesses to the same overt Act, or on Confession in open Court.

The Congress shall have Power to declare the Punishment of Treason, but no Attainder of Treason shall work Corruption of Blood, or Forfeiture except during the Life of the Person attainted.

## ARTICLE IV

## SECTION 1

Full Faith and Credit shall be given in each State to the public Acts, Records, and judicial Proceedings of every other State. And the Congress may by general Laws prescribe the Manner in which such Acts, Records and Proceedings shall be proved, and the Effect thereof.

## SECTION 2

The Citizens of each State shall be entitled to all Privileges and Immunities of Citizens in the several States.

A Person charged in any State with Treason, Felony, or other Crime, who shall flee from Justice, and be found in another State, shall on Demand of the executive Authority of the State from which he fled, be delivered up, to be removed to the State having Jurisdiction of the Crime.

No Person held to Service or Labour in one State, under the Laws thereof, escaping into another, shall, in Consequence of any Law or Regulation therein, be discharged from such Service or Labour, but shall be delivered up on Claim of the Party to whom such Service or Labour may be due.

## SECTION 3

New States may be admitted by the Congress into this Union; but no new State shall be formed or erected within the Jurisdiction of any other State; nor any State be formed by the Junction of two or more States, or Parts of States, without the Consent of the Legislatures of the States concerned as well as of the Congress.

The Congress shall have Power to dispose of and make all needful Rules and Regulations respecting the Territory, or other Property belonging to the United States; and nothing in this Constitution shall be so construed as to Prejudice any Claims of the United States, or of any particular State.

## SECTION 4

The United States shall guarantee to every State in this Union a Republican Form of Government, and shall protect each of them against Invasion; and on Application of the Legislature, or of the Executive (when the Legislature cannot be convened) against domestic Violence.

# ARTICLE V

The Congress, whenever two thirds of both Houses shall deem it necessary, shall propose Amendments to this Constitution, or, on the Application of the Legislatures of two thirds of the several States, shall call a Convention for proposing Amendments, which, in either Case, shall be valid to all Intents and Purposes, as Part of this Constitution, when ratified by the Legislatures of three fourths of the several States, or by Conventions in three fourths thereof, as the one or the other Mode of Ratification may be proposed by the Congress; Provided that no Amendment which may be made prior to the Year One thousand eight hundred and eight shall in any Manner affect the first and fourth Clauses in the Ninth Section of the first Article; and that no State, without its Consent, shall be deprived of its equal Suffrage in the Senate.

# ARTICLE VI

## SECTION 1

All Debts contracted and Engagements entered into, before the Adoption of this Constitution, shall be as valid against the United States under this Constitution, as under the Confederation.

## SECTION 2

This Constitution, and the Laws of the United States which shall be made in Pursuance thereof; and all Treaties made, or which shall be made, under the Authority of the United States, shall be the supreme Law of the Land; and the Judges in every State shall be bound thereby, any Thing in the Constitution or Laws of any State to the Contrary notwithstanding.

## SECTION 3

The Senators and Representatives before mentioned, and the Members of the several State Legislatures, and all executive and judicial Officers, both of the United States and of the several States, shall be bound by Oath or Affirmation, to support this Constitution; but no religious Test shall ever be required as a Qualification to any Office or public Trust under the United States.

# ARTICLE VII

The Ratification of the Conventions of nine States, shall be sufficient for the Establishment of this Constitution between the States so ratifying the Same.

DONE in Convention by the Unanimous Consent of the States present the Seventeenth Day of September in the Year of our Lord one thousand seven hundred and Eighty seven and of the Independance of the United States of America the Twelfth. IN WITNESS whereof We have hereunto subscribed our Names.

George Washington
   President and Deputy from
   Virginia

**NEW HAMPSHIRE**
John Langdon
Nicholas Gilman

**MASSACHUSETTS**
Nathaniel Gorman
Rufus King

**NEW YORK**
Alexander Hamilton

**NEW JERSEY**
William Livingston
David Brearley
William Paterson
Jonathan Dayton

**PENNSYLVANIA**
Benjamin Franklin
Thomas Mifflin
Robert Morris
George Clymer
Thomas FitzSimons
Jared Ingersoll

**DELAWARE**
George Read
Gunning Bedford, Jr.
John Dickinson
Richard Bassett
Jacob Broom

**MARYLAND**
James McHenry
Daniel of St. Thomas Jenifer
Daniel Carroll

**VIRGINIA**
John Blair
James Madison, Jr.

**NORTH CAROLINA**
William Blount
Richard Dobbs Spaight
Hugh Williamson

**SOUTH CAROLINA**
John Rutledge
Charles Cotesworth Pinckney
Charles Pinckney
Pierce Butler

**GEORGIA**
William Few
Abraham Baldwin

**CONNECTICUT**
William Samuel Johnson
Roger Sherman

# Amendments to the Constitution

## AMENDMENT I

Congress shall make no law respecting an establishment of religion, or prohibiting the free exercise thereof; or abridging the freedom of speech, or of the press; or the right of the people peaceably to assemble, and to petition the Government for a redress of grievances.

## AMENDMENT II

A well regulated Militia, being necessary to the security of a free State, the right of the people to keep and bear Arms, shall not be infringed.

## AMENDMENT III

No Soldier shall, in time of peace be quartered in any house, without the consent of the Owner, nor in time of war, but in a manner to be prescribed by law.

# AMENDMENT IV

The right of the people to be secure in their persons, houses, papers, and effects, against unreasonable searches and seizures, shall not be violated, and no Warrants shall issue, but upon probable cause, supported by Oath or affirmation, and particularly describing the place to be searched, and the persons or things to be seized.

# AMENDMENT V

No person shall be held to answer for a capital, or otherwise infamous crime, unless on a presentment or indictment of a Grand Jury, except in cases arising in the land or naval forces, or in the Militia, when in actual service in time of War or public danger; nor shall any person be subject for the same offence to be twice put in jeopardy of life or limb; nor shall be compelled in any criminal case to be a witness against himself, nor be deprived of life, liberty, or property, without due process of law; nor shall private property be taken for public use, without just compensation.

# AMENDMENT VI

In all criminal prosecutions, the accused shall enjoy the right to a speedy and public trial, by an impartial jury of the State and district wherein the crime shall have been committed, which district shall have been previously ascertained by law, and to be informed of the nature and cause of the accusation; to be confronted with the witnesses against him; to have compulsory process for obtaining Witnesses in his favor, and to have the assistance of counsel for his defence.

# AMENDMENT VII

In Suits at common law, where the value in controversy shall exceed twenty dollars, the right of trial by jury shall be preserved, and no fact tried by a jury, shall be otherwise re-examined in any Court of the United States, than according to the rules of the common law.

# AMENDMENT VIII

Excessive bail shall not be required, nor excessive fines imposed, nor cruel and unusual punishments inflicted.

# AMENDMENT IX

The enumeration in the Constitution, of certain rights, shall not be construed to deny or disparage others retained by the people.

# AMENDMENT X

The powers not delegated to the United States by the Constitution, nor prohibited by it to the States, are reserved to the States respectively, or to the people.

# AMENDMENT XI

The Judicial power of the United States shall not be construed to extend to any suit in law or equity, commenced or prosecuted against one of the United States by Citizens of another State, or by Citizens or Subjects of any Foreign State.

# AMENDMENT XII

The Electors shall meet in their respective states, and vote by ballot for President and Vice-President, one of whom, at least, shall not be an inhabitant of the same state with themselves; they shall name in their ballots the person voted for as President, and in distinct ballots the person voted for as Vice-President, and they shall make distinct lists of all persons voted for as President, and of all persons voted for as Vice-President, and of the number of votes for each, which lists they shall sign and certify, and transmit sealed to the seat of the government of the United States, directed to the President of the Senate;—The President of the Senate shall, in the presence of the Senate and House of Representatives, open all the certificates and the votes shall then be counted;—The person having the greatest number of votes for President, shall be the President, if such number be a majority of the whole number of Electors appointed; and if no person have such majority, then from the persons having the highest numbers not exceeding three on the list of those voted for as President, the House of Representatives shall choose immediately, by ballot, the President. But in choosing the President, the votes shall be taken by states, the representation from each state having one vote; a quorum for this purpose shall consist of a member or members from two-thirds of the states, and a majority of all the states shall be necessary to a choice. And if the House of Representatives shall not choose a President whenever the right of choice shall devolve upon them, before the fourth day of March next following, then the Vice-President shall act as President, as in the case of the death or other constitutional disability of the President.—The person having the greatest number of votes as Vice-President, shall be the Vice-President, if such number be a majority of the whole number of Electors appointed, and if no person have a majority, then from the two highest numbers on the list, the Senate shall choose the Vice-President; a quorum for the purpose shall consist of two-thirds of the whole number of Senators, and a majority of the whole number shall be necessary to a choice. But no person constitutionally ineligible to the office of President shall be eligible to that of Vice-President of the United States.

# AMENDMENT XIII

## SECTION 1

Neither slavery nor involuntary servitude, except as a punishment for crime whereof the party shall have been duly convicted, shall exist within the United States, or any place subject to their jurisdiction.

## SECTION 2

Congress shall have power to enforce this article by appropriate legislation.

# AMENDMENT XIV

## SECTION 1

All persons born or naturalized in the United States, and subject to the jurisdiction thereof, are citizens of the United States and of the State wherein they reside. No State shall make or enforce any law which shall abridge the privileges or immunities of citizens of the United States; nor shall any State deprive any person of life, liberty, or property, without due process of law; nor deny to any person within its jurisdiction the equal protection of the laws.

## SECTION 2

Representatives shall be apportioned among the several States according to their respective numbers, counting the whole number of persons in each State, excluding Indians not taxed. But when the right to vote at any election for the choice of electors for President and Vice President of the United States, Representatives in Congress, the Executive and Judicial officers of a State, or the members of the Legislature thereof, is denied to any of the male inhabitants of such State, being twenty-one years of age, and citizens of the United States, or in any way abridged, except for participation in rebellion, or other crime, the basis of representation therein shall be reduced in the proportion which the number of such male citizens shall bear to the whole number of male citizens twenty-one years of age in such State.

## SECTION 3

No person shall be a Senator or Representative in Congress, or elector of President and Vice President, or hold any office, civil or military, under the United States, or under any State, who, having previously taken an oath, as a member of Congress, or as an officer of the United States, or as a member of any State legislature, or as an executive or judicial officer of any State, to support the Constitution of the United States, shall have engaged in insurrection or rebellion against the same, or given aid or comfort to the enemies thereof. But Congress may by a vote of two-thirds of each House, remove such disability.

## SECTION 4

The validity of the public debt of the United States, authorized by law, including debts incurred for payment of pensions and bounties for services in suppressing insurrection or rebellion, shall not be questioned. But neither the United States nor any State shall assume or pay any debt or obligation incurred in aid of insurrection or rebellion against the United States, or any claim for the loss or emancipation of any slave; but all such debts, obligations and claims shall be held illegal and void.

## SECTION 5

The Congress shall have power to enforce, by appropriate legislation, the provisions of this article.

# AMENDMENT XV

## SECTION 1

The right of citizens of the United States to vote shall not be denied or abridged by the United States or by any State on account of race, color, or previous condition of servitude.

## SECTION 2

The Congress shall have power to enforce this article by appropriate legislation.

# AMENDMENT XVI

The Congress shall have power to lay and collect taxes on incomes, from whatever source derived, without apportionment among the several States, and without regard to any census or enumeration.

# AMENDMENT XVII

The Senate of the United States shall be composed of two Senators from each State, elected by the people thereof, for six years; and each Senator shall have one vote. The electors in each State shall have the qualifications requisite for electors of the most numerous branch of the State legislatures.

When vacancies happen in the representation of any State in the Senate, the executive authority of such State shall issue writs of election to fill such vacancies: Provided, That the legislature of any State may empower the executive thereof to make temporary appointments until the people fill the vacancies by election as the legislature may direct.

This amendment shall not be so construed as to affect the election or term of any Senator chosen before it becomes valid as part of the Constitution.

# AMENDMENT XVIII

## SECTION 1

After one year from the ratification of this article the manufacture, sale, or transportation of intoxicating liquors within, the importation thereof into, or the exportation thereof from the United States and all territory subject to the jurisdiction thereof for beverage purposes is hereby prohibited.

## SECTION 2

The Congress and the several States shall have concurrent power to enforce this article by appropriate legislation.

## SECTION 3

This article shall be inoperative unless it shall have been ratified as an amendment to the Constitution by the legislatures of the several States, as provided in the Constitution, within seven years from the date of the submission hereof to the States by the Congress.

# AMENDMENT XIX

The right of citizens of the United States to vote shall not be denied or abridged by the United States or by any State on account of sex.

Congress shall have power to enforce this article by appropriate legislation.

# AMENDMENT XX

## SECTION 1

The terms of the President and Vice President shall end at noon on the 20th day of January, and the terms of Senators and Representatives at noon on the 3d day of January, of the years in which such terms would have ended if this article had not been ratified; and the terms of their successors shall then begin.

## SECTION 2

The Congress shall assemble at least once in every year, and such meeting shall begin at noon on the 3d day of January, unless they shall by law appoint a different day.

## SECTION 3

If, at the time fixed for the beginning of the term of the President, the President elect shall have died, the Vice President elect shall become President. If a President shall not have been chosen before the time fixed for the beginning of his term, or if the President elect shall have failed to qualify, then the Vice President elect shall act as President until a President shall have qualified; and the Congress may by law provide for the case wherein neither a President elect nor a Vice President elect shall have qualified, declaring who shall then act as President, or the manner in which one who is to act shall be selected, and such person shall act accordingly until a President or Vice President shall have qualified.

## SECTION 4

The Congress may by law provide for the case of the death of any of the persons from whom the House of Representatives may choose a President whenever the right of choice shall have devolved upon them, and for the case of the death of any of the persons from whom the Senate may choose a Vice President whenever the right of choice shall have devolved upon them.

## SECTION 5

Sections 1 and 2 shall take effect on the 15th day of October following the ratification of this article.

## SECTION 6

This article shall be inoperative unless it shall have been ratified as an amendment to the Constitution by the legislatures of three-fourths of the several States within seven years from the date of its submission.

# AMENDMENT XXI

## SECTION 1

The eighteenth article of amendment to the Constitution of the United States is hereby repealed.

## SECTION 2

The transportation or importation into any State, Territory, or possession of the United States for delivery or use therein of intoxicating liquors, in violation of the laws thereof, is hereby prohibited.

## SECTION 3

This article shall be inoperative unless it shall have been ratified as an amendment to the Constitution by conventions in the several States, as provided in the Constitution, within seven years from the date of the submission hereof to the States by the Congress.

# AMENDMENT XXII

## SECTION 1

No person shall be elected to the office of the President more than twice, and no person who has held the office of President, or acted as President, for more than two years of a term to which some other person was elected President shall be elected to the office of the President more than once. But this Article shall not apply to any person holding the office of President when this Article was proposed by the Congress, and shall not prevent any person who may be holding the office of President, or acting as President, during the term within which this Article becomes operative from holding the office of President or acting as President during the remainder of such term.

## SECTION 2

This article shall be inoperative unless it shall have been ratified as an amendment to the Constitution by the legislatures of three-fourths of the several states within seven years from the date of its submission to the states by the Congress.

# AMENDMENT XXIII

## SECTION 1

The District constituting the seat of government of the United States shall appoint in such manner as the Congress may direct:

A number of electors of President and Vice President equal to the whole number of Senators and Representatives in Congress to which the District would be entitled if it were a state, but in no event more than the least populous State; they shall be in addition to those appointed by the States, but they shall be considered, for the purposes of the election of President and Vice President, to be electors appointed by a State; and they shall meet in the District and perform such duties as provided by the twelfth article of amendment.

## SECTION 2

The Congress shall have power to enforce this article by appropriate legislation.

# AMENDMENT XXIV

## SECTION 1

The right of citizens of the United States to vote in any primary or other election for President or Vice President, for electors for President or Vice President, or for Senator or Representative in Congress, shall not be denied or abridged by the United States or any State by reason of failure to pay any poll tax or other tax.

## SECTION 2

The Congress shall have power to enforce this article by appropriate legislation.

# AMENDMENT XXV

## SECTION 1

In case of the removal of the President from office or of his death or resignation, the Vice President shall become President.

## SECTION 2

Whenever there is a vacancy in the office of the Vice President, the President shall nominate a Vice President who shall take office upon confirmation by a majority vote of both Houses of Congress.

## SECTION 3

Whenever the President transmits to the President pro tempore of the Senate and the Speaker of the House of Representatives his written declaration that he is unable to discharge the powers and duties of his office, and until he transmits to them a written declaration to the contrary, such powers and duties shall be discharged by the Vice President as Acting President.

## SECTION 4

Whenever the Vice President and a majority of either the principal officers of the executive departments or of such other body as Congress may by law provide, transmit to the President pro tempore of the Senate and the Speaker of the House of Representatives their written declaration that the President is unable to discharge the powers and duties of his office, the Vice President shall immediately assume the powers and duties of the office as Acting President.

Thereafter, when the President transmits to the President pro tempore of the Senate and the Speaker of the House of Representatives his written declaration that no inability exists, he shall resume the powers and duties of his office unless the Vice President and a majority of either the principal officers of the executive department or of such other body as Congress may by law provide, transmit within four days to the President pro tempore of the Senate and the Speaker of the House of Representatives their written declaration that the President is unable to discharge the powers and duties of his office. Thereupon Congress shall decide the issue, assembling within forty-eight hours for that purpose if not in session. If the Congress, within twenty-one days after receipt of the latter written declaration, or, if Congress is not in session, within twenty-one days after Congress is required to assemble, determines by two-thirds vote of both Houses that the President is unable to discharge the powers and duties of his office, the Vice President shall continue to discharge the same as Acting President; otherwise, the President shall resume the powers and duties of his office.

# AMENDMENT XXVI

## SECTION 1

The right of citizens of the United States, who are eighteen years of age or older, to vote, shall not be denied or abridged by the United States or by any State on account of age.

## SECTION 2

The Congress shall have power to enforce this article by appropriate legislation.

# AMENDMENT XXVII

No law varying the compensation for the services of the senators and representatives shall take effect, until an election of representatives shall have intervened.

# Statement Submitted by
# John Benson Bancroft and Gail Jean Yax
# Troy High School, Troy, Michigan

## to the U.S. Senate Committee on Health, Education, Labor and Pensions

*Hearing on School Safety: Intervention and Prevention Strategies*
*May 6, 1999*

Mr. Chairman, my name is John Bancroft, and I am a lifetime resident of the state of Michigan. My statement today is submitted on behalf of myself, my colleague, Gail Yax, and, most importantly, the students of Troy High School in Troy, Michigan. Together we have implemented a very successful conflict resolution, peer mediation program. It has been widely shared in our state and is deemed a "model" in school violence prevention. Our program has been presented to schoolwide assemblies and we have produced videos; made presentations to parent groups, administrative personnel, school boards, middle schools and teachers and counselors around the state.

As is customary, I would like to take a moment to briefly share with the members of the Committee a little background about myself and Gail Yax. I earned my bachelor's degree in geography and history at Michigan State University. My 30-year teaching career has been spent entirely at Troy High School in Troy, Michigan. Troy High School is home to 2000 students and flies 30+ international flags proudly representing its diverse population. In addition to classroom work, often with at-risk students, I coached varsity track for 26 years including a national champion and 18 All-State athletes. I also had the honor of being named Coach of the Year several times. Although I have always loved coaching kids in sports and games, my passion has become coaching kids in life—how to live it and love it!

Gail Yax has a bachelor's and master's degree in business and is near completion of a master's in counseling and clinical psychology. She has taught for 20 years and chairs her department. Gail, too, has a good deal of experience with at-risk students. I would like to add that her father was a Highland Park police officer, which provides her with a deep and very personal understanding of the impact of violence on young lives. Gail is a second generation Syrian-American.

Our interest and work in diversity training and peer mediation over the past several years grew out of personal and professional observations and realizations that past perceptions and norms are no longer valid in today's schools. Therefore, past methods, past "remedies" will no longer work. If we are to ensure this nation's future, our young people must be allowed to feel safe and, indeed, should EXPECT to feel safe in a wholesome, educational environment. If we are committed to our future, change is not only important, it is imperative.

With that having been said, Mr. Chairman, in light of the tragic events that have occurred in Littleton, Colorado, we feel compelled to tell our story. The students' appearance and demeanor at Columbine High School reminded us of our students at Troy High School. The school and community in Littleton seem very similar to the upscale suburban population of our Troy community. As we watched that now so infamous tragedy unfold on national television, both teachers and students were forced to compare our own experiences to theirs. As previously stated, since we were so shocked by the similarities between the two communities, we felt compelled to tell our story. We are convinced that our experiences and the peer mediation model that we use at Troy High School can help other high schools deal with the troubles that concern our whole nation.

We would like to convey our strong support of the Committee's efforts to find a way to bring an end to the school violence that is showing up all too often in our schools across the country. We are confident that we as a nation can meet the challenge before us. If fear and doubt freeze our ability to act, history will record that our nation could not create a safe environment for our children. This cannot and should not be our legacy!

Nine years ago, Troy High School was having some serious problems. A high-profile athlete was arrested for trafficking cocaine. Parents, teachers, administrators and coaches had noticed that his attitude was declining, but we never suspected drugs, much less drug trafficking! When we returned from summer vacation and read the newspaper headlines, "Troy High School Athlete Arrested in Drug Case," we were in shock. How could this happen in our school? Why didn't even one student come to us and suggest that there was a problem?

About the same time, two Asian girls came to us and alleged that they had been spit upon and called derogatory names. Further, at this time, the war with Iraq was raging and ethnic tension and intimidation became part of our daily lives. Prejudices were exploding between Chaldean students and students identified as athletes. One Chaldean student told us that he did not think he would finish the year if the "pressure did not stop." Our African American students were "just not feeling part of the school" in some instances. Several fights broke out in school, talk of retaliation and weapons was buzzing around the halls, and although we tried suspensions and expulsions, we couldn't resolve our problems and refocus on learning.

Troy High School was and is an award-winning high school. We, for the most part, have highly motivated and successful students. We also have very good parental support and a very professional staff of teachers and administrators. We had always used fair and reasonable discipline. So how was this going on beneath our noses? We were going about our business in a very professional way and still these problems continued to happen. We began to ask ourselves, what dynamics were behind these unacceptable events? Communication between students and adults was lacking. I guess you might say, this was our "wake-up call."

In 1991, after a fight in the hallway between Chaldean students and other students, tensions were very high. On one particular Friday evening, I had a difficult time sleeping. I was afraid something bad was going to happen in school. The next morning, I called the school board president and asked to meet for a cup of coffee and talk. I described my firsthand experiences, observations and fears. I told her that either the adults did not know about the potential problems or did not know what to do about them. I felt we were looking at another case where we would react only after tragedy. The school board president assured me that the board and administration would support a group of 10 teachers to interview student groups. This process started in the spring of 1991 and continued throughout 1992. Many concerns were relayed from the students to the committee that was ultimately composed of seven teachers, one social worker, one administrator and one school board member. Because Troy High is one of the most ethnically diverse high schools in the nation, the committee focused on multicultural problems and began a two-year effort to increase ethnic understanding. We did increase ethnic understanding but that did little to reduce conflict.

In 1993, two boys, one Chaldean and one "white," exchanged words including racial insults. The "white" student, fearing a beating, later came into the school with an iron pipe and hit the Chaldean boy in the face. In an instant, students were rushing out of the doors and into the parking lot. By the time staff rushed to the parking lot to intervene, many fights had broken out. One teacher was knocked to the pavement and another had his shirt ripped off. Several boys were bloodied and many students were very emotional. Blood was spilled, students were suspended and we barely missed the headlines. Now we realize that our multicultural approach would not resolve the conflict. This was disappointing after three years of real effort to resolve these problems.

Then in 1994, my colleague, Gail Yax, had an important insight which helped us to turn the corner. She suggested that part of the problem may be that we were treating our conflicts as just that, conflict. We would take the focus off of race, jocks, drugs, weirdness, etc.

Diversity is our nation's greatest strength. By focusing on things like race, religion, sex, ethnicity, nerds, geeks, athletes, etc., when there is conflict, it makes these diversities a negative. Conflict is part of life. Conflict is normal. Conflict can be good. Looking at conflict as conflict and not as an ethnic problem takes the attention off of ethnicity and onto resolution. Treating conflict actually reduces the tension that normally surrounds it. In the last five years, we feel that we have made great strides into these problems by implementing Peer Mediation.

Working together with the Troy Community Coalition and the Michigan Law Related Education Project, we enlisted help from the Cleveland Marshall School of Law. Trainers from the Cleveland Marshall School of Law came to our school and talked to a group of staff members. We picked 30 students that first year and spent two days being trained by these experts. Since that training session five years ago, we have modified the original program to meet the needs of our school. We now train approximately 130 students per year and also have trained over 30 teachers and administrators.

As of May 1999, we have done over 120 mediations with many more informal personal contacts. I have one mediation hour in the lunchroom and during that time, many students approach me with school-related concerns. Every year in the fall, Gail Yax and I train all the mediators for two full days. Again in the spring they are taken out of the school for a day of refresher training . . . . During mediations, the disputants also learn the process by being active participants.

Our beautiful city is not immune from some very tragic events that you would not expect in an affluent city like Troy. Let me relate one story to you. One senior mediator was given the job of organizing a mediation for two girls who exchanged punches in the hallway. They were sent home for the day to "cool off." Upon returning to school the next day, they were required to go to mediation. The fight was over rumors. The first attempt to mediate this conflict ended in an impasse. The student mediator then took each girl alone to talk.

One girl was depressed because her sister had been murdered in another city the year before in a drive-by shooting. She was first-generation Rumanian. Her friends in the school wanted to put flowers by her deceased sister's old locker. There was a misunderstanding and an administrator took the flowers away from the locker. This act caused hard feelings with the students. The Rumanian girls and her friends felt that "Rumanians don't count at Troy High." Her anger had evolved into depression. She felt that nobody cared for her or understood her. The other girl in the dispute revealed to Val that her father had held a gun to her head and called her a "slut." She also revealed that her mother said that she was cursed when she was born. This young lady was ultimately referred to the school social worker for further assistance.

The mediator brought them back together and told them that they had no reason to hate each other. What they hated were the traits of their lives they shared! They talked to each other about their life stories. When they saw how much they had in common they did not want to fight. The unacceptable conditions that existed before peer mediation ceased to exist.

Communication is opening up. There is never a moment in our school that some kind of peer mediation or discussion on resolving conflict is not going on. We are not afraid to let the students confront one another with their problems and help to resolve them. With these mechanisms in place, we cannot imagine a tragedy happening without us knowing first about the potential for trouble with time to work toward a resolution. Administrators and teachers still discipline students. However, students resolve most of the disputes; those problems that arise without anyone knowing are very rare.

Beside the mediation process itself, what other benefits do we gain by creating a conflict resolution program? One young woman spent most of her freshman and sophomore years in conflict with other students, ultimately being suspended for fighting. Her self-esteem was low and she was mediated approximately 10 times. One day, she came to us and asked if she could become a mediator because she knew firsthand that it worked! She became one of our best! While she is by no means out of the woods, she is on a path that can lead her out.

We had another tough character who bullied and terrorized other students for two years. He was suspended several times for fighting. One of the mediators recommended that we train him.

Because of the respect of classmates, he has completed several successful mediations this year. This same young man put himself on the line when a Filipino student was getting pelted by snowballs in the parking lot after school . . . . The Filipino student got out of his car and confronted the mob of boys throwing the snowballs at his car. Another boy stepped forward and a fight broke out. The Filipino's sister got out of the car to help her brother. They were both knocked to the ground and 10-12 boys started kicking them. This is where the former fighter, turned mediator, stepped in. Rather than reverting back to old habits and joining the fight, he brought it to a halt. Other mediators joined in to disburse the crowd and avert the potential for serious injury. Not only were five suspensions the result but a pat on the back for the young mediator who took the risk not only to change his behavior but to be a model for others. We do not tell the peer mediators to break up altercations, but some people are by nature people of action and it is better to take positive action than negative.

We have also done a good number of mediations relating to threats, insults and rumors being sent over computers. One comes to mind where two boys were making death threats back and forth with e-mail.

Watching the coverage of the Colorado tragedy, two issues have been repeated: some students feel alienated and some feel left out. Schools have always had students that have felt this way. Maybe today these feelings are stronger and some students are not acting on their feelings. It is important that all human beings feel wanted as part of the human race.

This brings to mind another example, that of a talented football player, by size and demeanor, an imposing young man. A jock acting as a mediator has a real impact and makes a real statement. He worked with two troubled girls who felt harassed by some immature boys. One girl had actually brought physical harm to herself, carving "I Hate God" in her leg with a knife. This young man and other mediators worked hard to get her back to her counselor and back on track. To see a popular jock sincerely trying to help students who are on the outside of the in-crowd solve a personal problem is a powerful message of tolerance and understanding.

Without this program, just because of his imposing size and being stereotyped as football jock, those girls might have assumed that he was just another jock. It is reassuring to the student body that this school leader is not only a good sport but a good person as well who took a personal interest in the well-being of a less fortunate peer.

Another senior sat down with some boys recently. One boy had his shoes stolen at a party, and five others from the party said they had no idea what happened. The boy's dad told his son to get the shoes back or he was going to call the police. This act would have created multiple problems for his son and may have resulted in trouble at school. The mediator said he would try to get the boys to work it out. He had the boy who lost the shoes and each one of the accused talk together privately. He got no movement. Then he brought the whole group together. After two hours, no one admitted to the theft, but they agreed to buy a new pair of shoes if the shoes did not "turn up." The mediator thought that the boys took the shoes but by this mediated solution we avoided problems which could have escalated into violence.

I feel that conflict resolution should become a way of life. The safety and emotional concerns of our students must come first. Intellectual concerns are easy when the students are safe and comfortable in the school. They become difficult when that security is lost. Peer mediation promotes safety, allowing students to arrive at their own solutions. They learn how to own their lives.

Gail Yax and I tried to pick our mediators from school and team leaders, from all groups, cliques and walks of life in our school. Our mediators reflect the diversity of our population at Troy High School and that is why we currently have in excess of 130 mediators. This gives us the flexibility to correctly match mediators to the situation with which they are confronted. Over 400 students applied to be peer mediators this year.

We also had an issue where two girls felt they were being made fun of by some boys. They felt hurt and fearful. This time four mediators sat down with the girls and talked over their concerns.

After a frustrating attempt to mediate the problem, the mediation ended in an impasse. Dismissing the mediation, a popular female mediator in the group sat for an hour talking with the girls. The act of understanding and acceptance by this particular student caused the other girls not to feel so isolated in the school. They all came to know one another better. Often after mediation, the mediators express the fact that they did not know that people had those kinds of problems. It gets both the mediators and the mediated to walk in each other's shoes.

To young people, it seems that violence is acceptable if nothing is done to end it. We have first to understand the problems in our schools and then attempt to do something about the violent results of those problems. We have spent 10 years at Troy High School working to find a way to reduce the conflict that is part of our children's everyday lives. Much time and energy have been spent to communicate with young people to find an answer.

We have seen the violence firsthand and a national effort is needed to rescue many of our soon-to-be young citizens. Sometimes even those who appear to be doing fine are not. When we are confronted by national emergencies, the federal government has always led the way. Sometimes it takes time for the government to get involved. The depression was devastating to the nation before FDR led us out. Pearl Harbor had to be bombed before we saved the world, and many people had to die in the south before the federal government stepped in and passed civil rights laws.

I believe in local control, but we need leadership from all levels of our government. If the violence that has been ravaging our country for decades had been perpetrated by a foreign power, we would have rallied all of our resources to fight this power. Dedicated educators have been up against this problem for years and, in some cases, are being worn down. Our schools need your continued support. WE NEED YOUR COMMITMENT NOW.

There is a little bit of good in the worst person and a little bit of bad in the best. Trying to identify a student who might do a bad thing is difficult. Chances of identifying potential problems are better if students are part of the process and are talking to classmates on a regular basis. With a peer mediation program in existence, students get used to looking for problems to solve and other students look to the peers for help.

Mr. Chairman, I hope that the Committee will take an interest in this conflict resolution, peer mediation model. I deeply appreciate this opportunity to describe how this program works and how others may benefit from it.

It is time to do something. Helping others to make our nation's schools a better and safer place for our children is not only important, it's the patriotic thing to do! Our peer mediation motto at Troy High School are the words of Martin Luther King, Jr. "Violence is the Language of the Unheard."

We are listening.

Thank you, Mr. Chairman.